PRESENTED TO

_____

FROM

_____

DATE

_____

from a Father's Heart

Letters of Encouragement to
Children and Grandchildren

D A N R E I L A N D

THOMAS NELSON PUBLISHERS
Nashville

Published in Nashville, Tennessee, by Thomas Nelson, Inc.

Unless otherwise noted, the Bible version used in this publication is THE NEW KING JAMES VERSION. Copyright © 1979, 1980, 1982, Thomas Nelson, Inc., Publishers.

The Scripture quotation noted PHILLIPS is from J. B. Phillips: THE NEW TESTAMENT IN MODERN ENGLISH. Revised Edition. Copyright © J. B. Phillips 1958, 1960, 1972. Used by permission of Macmillan Publishing Co., Inc.

The Scripture quotation noted RSV is from the REVISED STANDARD VERSION of the Bible. Copyright © 1946, 1952, 1971, 1973 by the Division of Christian Education of the National Council of the Churches of Christ in the U.S.A. Used by permission.

Cover and Interior Design: Big Picture / D2 DesignWorks
Photography: Tony Stone Images

Library of Congress Cataloging-in-Publication Data
Reiland, Dan.
      From a father's heart : letters of encouragement to children and
   grandchildren / Dan Reiland.
            p. cm.
      ISBN 0-7852-7043-4 (hc)
            1. Father and child—Correspondence. 2. Grandfathers—Correspondence.
   3. Grandparent and child—Correspondence. 4. Parenting—Religious aspects—
   Christianity. 5. Grandparenting—Religious aspects—Christianity. I. Title.
   HQ755.85.R435 1999
   306.874'2—dc21

                                                                98-48625

                                                            CIP

Printed in the United States of America.

   2 3 4 5 6 — 04 03 02 01 00 99

To

RAY "DAD" CROWELL

The dad who invested deeply and richly in my life.

————

And to my beautiful children,

MACKENZIE ANN-MARIE

AND JOHN-PETER.

My great joy is to be your dad!

Contents

Acknowledgments

Patti Reiland | Typing, typing, and more typing! Thank you for your flying fingers, great proofreading, and loving support. And most of all, thank you for being the *great* mom of the kids my letters are written to.

Tami McCarthy | Thank you for doing the "first edits" while home-schooling three kids; juggling a few hundred household chores; chasing two dogs, a few birds, and other stray animals; and keeping track of Marv.

Victor Oliver | Thank you for giving this book an opportunity, and for your wise coaching and creative ideas.

Brian Hampton | Thank you, as managing editor, for your servant spirit and commitment to excellence.

Stephanie Wolfe | Thank you for keeping my professional life organized so that I could "create" time to write this book!

John Maxwell | Thank you for sharing your friends with me. Their letters are great!

And to the dads who said yes when I asked them to write a letter for this book, I am sincerely grateful for your generous contribution.

Introduction

Kids are wonderful. But if you have been a parent for more than a few days, you know that parenting can be very challenging at times!

Kids grow up fast. In the hustle and bustle of life, parents and grandparents can get caught up in the demands of each day. Full schedules often leave too little time and energy for instilling our most cherished values in our children. Before we know it, our kids are grown and gone. That is part of what motivated me to design and write this book. My desire is to serve you, not by telling you what is important but by offering you a selection of values to read about so you can determine which ones resonate in your heart as true and important.

This collection of letters contains life principles that are birthed in the heart and come from real family situations. The letters can help you as a parent or grandparent in many ways. You may wish to read the letters to your kids and then talk about them together. You may wish to use them as examples so you can write your own letters. You may even want to ask your kids to read the letters on their own and then tell you what they think about them and what they learned from them. Whichever method you choose, remember that discussion is the key to making the principles in these letters come alive in your family.

Kids are our future. My hope and desire is that this book will help you shape your child's or grandchild's future in a positive and productive way.

Dan Reiland

Of all nature's gifts to the human race,

what is sweeter
to a man than his children?

Cicero

Oak Trees and Eagles | Dan Reiland

Dear Mackenzie and John-Peter,

Oak trees and eagles are about roots and wings, two of the most fundamental things I can give you as you grow up. It's my heart's desire to give you both.

Oak trees have roots that go deep into the ground. They provide strength to hold the mighty oak steady through even the worst of storms. The roots also pull food and water out of the soil to nourish the tree day after day, month after month, year after year. Without the roots the oak could not stand. I am helping you plant your roots deep and secure so that you may stand strong, no matter how hard the winds of life may blow. The principles in these letters, which we have talked about and will talk about many times in the future, will help you develop your roots.

Eagles are magnificent creatures that do not follow a flock, but lead the way as they soar high above the trees in all their splendor. Eagles are beautiful and graceful. They are strong and capable. Eagles are often associated with success. That is how I see you in the future, as eagles, the best, at the top, capable, strong, beautiful, and graceful in your adult years. You will achieve great heights and fear nothing. For now, however, even baby eagles need a push. I want to give you just enough of a loving push in life that you may soar to your maximum potential. From now until the time when you fly on your own, I will do my best to be the wind beneath your wings.

I love you deeply and I believe in you.

Your dad

I am helping you plant your roots deep and secure so that you may stand strong.

God Room | Franklin Graham

President, Samaritan's Purse; Boone, North Carolina
Written to his four children, Will, Edward, Roy, and Cissie

Dear kids,

Your mother and I can hardly believe how fast time has gone by since you were born. It seems as though it was just yesterday that we brought you home from the hospital all wrapped up in a tiny bundle of blankets.

Many times I've wondered if our home was big enough for all four of you kids and your dogs, cats, birds, and other critters. Now I realize it won't be too long before you all will be leaving home—for college, for marriage, for service to God. I know the Lord has a wonderful plan for each of you, and He will bring that plan to successful completion.

I was twenty-three—just about your age, Will—when I learned a spiritual lesson that helped shape my life. It's something that I want to pass on to all of you. I'm talking about the principle of "God room," a lesson taught to me by Dr. Bob Pierce, the founder of Samaritan's Purse.

As you know, Dr. Bob devoted his life to meeting the physical needs of the hurting and downtrodden in order to show them God's love and earn a hearing for the gospel. He would go to the most desperate places on earth, find out how he could help people there, then share those needs with people who could pray and give in support of his efforts. No need was ever too big for Dr. Bob to tackle, not because he had great resources, but because he practiced "God room."

Dr. Bob explained "God room" to me this way. "Buddy," he said, "when you see a need that God wants you to meet, and all that you can do to meet that need is still not enough,

5

Don't be afraid to accept challenges that God sends your way that are too big for you.

then you're operating in 'God room.' That's when you pray and leave room for God to work. If you can meet the need yourself, God doesn't have to do anything. But when it's bigger than your abilities and your resources, God has room to work. That's when things get exciting."

That simple principle has stuck with me, and I have found it to be true time and time again. When Dr. Bob died in 1978, the Samaritan's Purse board of directors asked me to be president. I knew that the challenge was bigger than I could handle on my own. But I also knew that if I were willing to operate in "God room," then God Himself would be at

work for the honor of Christ. And that's exactly what has happened. God has done more than I could ever imagine, and I give Him the praise and glory.

I've met other servants of Christ around the world who understand and live by this principle. You've been to the Annoor Sanatorium for Chest Diseases in Mafraq, Jordan, where the bedouins come to receive treatment for tuberculosis and other illnesses. When I helped with the construction of that hospital as a teenager, I saw Dr. Eleanor Soltau and nurse Aileen Coleman practice "God room" over and over again. The only way those two women were able to establish a Christian ministry in the

Muslim world was to take on challenges too big for them, then trust God to work.

Pastor Sami Dagher in Beirut, Lebanon, is another example of someone who operates in "God room." During those awful years when Beirut was blown to bits by war, he never shrank from the challenges of ministering in Christ's name, even when he was surrounded by bullets, rockets, car bombs, and kidnappings. He could have left Lebanon for an easier life anytime he wanted—but he chose to stay and give God the opportunity to work through him. Today his church is a shining light for Christ, not only in Beirut but across the Middle East.

My point in writing is to encourage you to live by the "God room" principle. Don't be afraid to accept challenges that God sends your way that are too big for you. Instead take on those challenges, relying humbly upon Him to do what He wants done.

God's Word puts it this way:

Trust in the LORD with all your heart,
And lean not on your own understanding;
In all your ways acknowledge Him,
And He shall direct your paths.
Do not be wise in your own eyes;
Fear the LORD and depart from evil.
It will be health to your flesh,
And strength to your bones. (Prov. 3:5–8)

When you live this way, I guarantee you, things will be exciting. And you may even find that living by "God room" gives you enough room in your own home one day for lots of kids and critters. When that happens, your mother and I will rejoice . . . and we will check into a hotel when we visit.

Love,
Dad

Time—A Precious Gift | Dan Reiland

Dear Mackenzie and John-Peter,

When you were younger, you would constantly ask on a trip, "Are we there yet?" We weren't in the air or down the road five minutes before you'd ask, "Are we there yet?" You had no concept of time then. And now that you understand time well, you're beginning to look at it as I do. It seems like there isn't enough time in the day to get everything done.

I don't want to talk to you about time management, which is a very important topic, because you can buy good books on that sub-

ject. I do want to talk to you about the *value* of time and the difference between using it wisely and wasting it. You are never too young or too old to learn these principles, but many people wait until they are old and are very disappointed with how they have used their time. When you are young, you believe you will live forever, but you won't. That may sound like a terrible thing to tell a child, but these principles are not meant just for today. They are designed for a lifetime. Think of it in a positive way. One day you will be with Jesus forever—in heaven—just as Grammy is. What you do with the time between now and then is important.

Time is the one thing that everyone has in common. In every other way we are different from one another—where we are born, what kind of parents we have, our physical genetics, talents and gifts, weaknesses and shortcomings. But we all have exactly 168 hours a week to do with as we choose.

Time is a gift from God. Some people use up their minutes, days, and years but never really live. They waste the gift. Be grateful for this gift of time — of life itself. Show your gratitude for this gift by the ways you use your time.

The second thing to remember is that you have enough time. Every day I hear someone say, "I just don't have enough time to get everything done." Yes, he does! He is trying to do too much. I believe that God is wise enough not to require you to do more than He gave you enough hours in a day to accomplish. So, whenever you find yourself without enough time to get everything done, you are more than likely attempting to do things that God doesn't need you to do.

The Bible says that there is a time for everything:

When in doubt,
invest your time in people.
That is the only investment that matters.

A time to be born,
　　And a time to die;
A time to plant,
　　And a time to pluck what is planted;
A time to kill,
　　And a time to heal;
A time to break down,
　　And a time to build up;
A time to weep,
　　And a time to laugh;
A time to mourn,
　　And a time to dance;
A time to cast away stones,
　　And a time to gather stones;
A time to embrace,
　　And a time to refrain from embracing;
A time to gain,
　　And a time to lose;
A time to keep,
　　And a time to throw away;
A time to tear,
　　And a time to sew;
A time to keep silence,

And a time to speak;
A time to love,
　　And a time to hate;
A time of war,
　　And a time of peace. (Eccl. 3:2–8)

I've heard both of you say, "I don't have time to get all my homework done." Yes, you do. And this leads us to the next principle.

Pay now and play later. Playing is healthy and good, but playing before finishing the important things is not. It's like eating your vegetables first because there is always room for dessert. Have you ever noticed that when you eat dessert first, you are not hungry for dinner? My mom used to say, "No snacking before dinner. It will ruin your appetite." Dinner, however, never ruined my appetite for dessert. Now that is something we all love in our family. Mom loves carrot cake, I love chocolate chip cookies, Mackenzie, you love vanilla ice cream, and John-Peter, well, you love *anything* sweet! Even though we love the goodies, we eat dinner first. Why? Because that's what makes our bodies healthy and strong. (Strong enough to eat more dessert!) You get the idea. Always do what is important first, and there will always be time for fun and play. If you play first, you'll be amazed at how little you get done.

Last, time can be spent or time can be invested. Spending time is like letting the hose run in the street. The water runs down into the gutter and does no good. Investing time is like letting the water run from the hose into the flower bed. The flowers grow strong, healthy, and beautiful for us all to enjoy. Investing your time instead of spending it doesn't mean you should constantly work. You shouldn't. Rest, relaxation, and recreation are necessary, and life is too short not to have fun.

But when it's all said and done, investment is always the better way. And when in doubt, invest your time in people. That is the only investment that matters.

I'm investing my time while I write these letters to you kids. I could rest, play, or go out to a movie, but that will all pass. These letters will last. Our conversations about them as you grow older will last. You may pass on some of the principles and ideas to your kids. I want you to know my heart. There is no greater investment of my time than in the lives of both of you. You are more beautiful than the flowers, and I love watching you grow.

I love you.

Dad

Honesty in Front of Jesus | Jack Hayford, D.Lit.

Senior Pastor, The Church on the Way; Van Nuys, California
Written to his four children and ten grandchildren

Dear kids,

It has been about five months since Grandma (Great-Grandma) went home to heaven. I was thinking how each of you has had a way of bringing comfort to me since my mama has gone. Things different ones of you have said—about loving her so much and about missing her—have been very special to me.

I'm proud of each of you. It's clear that all of you—each in your own way—have a special place in your hearts for her because you value the kind of person she was. That reveals wisdom, genuine "smarts" on your part. I mean, in a day when too many kids your ages aren't sharp enough to recognize the blessing and beauty many older people have to offer, you're different—all of you. But then Grandma was pretty sharp herself, staying "forever young" even when she was in her eighties! You loved and liked each other—great kids and a grand grandma. I love to think about it. You deserved each other.

But I wrote to say more than how heart-warmed I am to think about all that. I really wanted to write a letter with a larger and longer issue in view—one I hope won't seem so "heavy" that it takes the edge off the "happy" I think you probably feel so far with this letter. I'm writing to talk about the greatest thing in the world when we think about a loved one dying: about how real heaven is, about how short life is, and about how often I think of wanting to be sure all of us are there together forever.

I'm glad I don't need to preach to you. If I did, I probably wouldn't write you about this because nothing is less productive than for relatives to "lay religion on" to other relatives. But the marvelous fact that each of you already knows the reality of our living Savior, Jesus, and that each one of you—on your own—has shown both the intelligence and the heart to put your faith in Him, makes it easy to write

friend's house—a kid named Chuck. The afternoon before, we had been goofing around in his room, and he had pulled out a tiny telescope he said his brother had given him. Well, it wasn't a telescope at all. When I peered into it, I saw the crude nude pornographic picture

Life really works only when we shoot straight with God.

this way. So I don't have a sermon, but I do have a story. It's about one of my longest-lasting memories of my mama, and how I think it can help all of us keep on-line with God so that none of us will miss the great reunion He has planned for all of us someday.

It happened when I was about eleven years old, pretty young, but still old enough to know when right's right and when wrong's wrong.

It was the morning after I'd been at a

fixed inside. I didn't want to seem out of it, so I laughed, even though inside my chest I felt something like a twinge of pain. (Isn't it funny how much we worry about what people think and we violate trust with our own hearts, trying to please someone we'll have so little to do with most of the rest of our lives? I haven't seen Chuck since I went to junior high.)

Anyway, the next day I was about to leave for school when my mama called me into the kitchen. "Jack," she said, "I want to ask you a question. But listen carefully, Son, because I'm asking you *in front of Jesus.*"

I felt as if my heart were about to stop. The few times she ever spoke those words, something real serious was up. I also knew when she said that, I couldn't really be anything but absolutely truthful—no matter what it cost. You see, early in my life, my mom and dad had helped me learn that you can never fake it with God. Looking back, I realize it may be one of the greatest gifts they gave me. Though I was always taught how much God really loves each one of us—which is, of course, why He gave us Jesus—I also learned His love calls for honesty. As Mama spoke, I sensed I was about to have to face up to truth I would rather avoid. And I was.

"Jack, *in front of Jesus,* what happened at Chuck's yesterday?" She explained how her heart had felt unexplainably heavy when I had come home the day before. After she had prayed for me and asked Father God why she

felt that way, she knew she was to simply ask me about the matter—*in front of Jesus.* Well, I told her what happened and, with sincere tears, asked her to pray with me. My inner sense of uncleanness left, and I was filled with the joyous, conscious, free peace we can all gain in *front of Jesus.* Minutes later I was on my way to school, relieved of a huge weight that had been lifted off my chest.

So, that's it—the memory I felt pretty sure you'd be interested to hear. Because you respected Grandma as much as you loved her, I thought you'd like the story behind a great life-secret she taught me. In short, it's that *life is a lot more fulfilling, and the heart is freer to be and keep happy, when we remain open and aboveboard with Christ.* I thought it worth sharing for another reason. If you know the story, maybe Grandma's great phrase will stick: *in front of Jesus.*

It was her way of reminding me that life really works only when we shoot straight with God. And I wanted to write you because I care so much that we all—each of us—keep "on-line" with heaven so we'll be "in line" when Father God calls us to His forever home. The sum of it all is simple: if we all live in front of Jesus here, we'll all meet in front of Jesus there. Nothing is more important to me than that happening, kids. And believe me, Grandma is waiting for it to happen too.

I love you—each one—a lot!

Dad—and Grandpa

Children's children are the crown of old men,
And the glory of children is their father.

Proverbs 17:6

Learning—A Lifetime Adventure | Dan Reiland

Dear Mackenzie and John-Peter,

In the summer of 1998 the news carried a story of Jeanie Garside, who graduated that summer from high school. What's so unusual? She was ninety-eight years old! Jeanie dropped out of elementary school at eight years old to help her parents care for the other eight kids. This was in Massachusetts in 1909. After a ninety-year break, she went back, studied, took her exams, and got her degree. After all that, she has considered college.

Going to school isn't a formula for success, but I'll tell you what is—learning and growing for a lifetime. School is where you begin to develop two important things: the value of discipline and the ability to think. If you get those two things under your belt, you have done well. If you have developed discipline in your life and have learned to think for yourself, you will be prepared for a lifetime of learning and growing.

If you stop learning, you stop growing, and if you stop growing—well, you just stop. Life gets dull and so do you. You don't have as much to give to others when you stop growing. Even when you finish college, you've just begun to learn what life has to teach you. The older I get and the more I learn, the more I realize I don't know. I still can't figure out how to operate the VCR!

Learn every day. I have the privilege to travel to many churches across the United States and Canada. In the past three years I have been to more than sixty churches, and I have learned something from every single one. Even the smallest and most humble churches have taught me something.

I was so proud of my mom (Grammy Betty). One year before she died, at sixty-six years old, she completed a six-week seminar on financial planning and money management for people over sixty-five. She kept learning and growing her entire life. She was just about to take her first computer course at sixty-seven years old.

In order to learn every day, you must set your mind on the task of learning something. It doesn't happen by accident. Ask questions. Develop relationships with many people who have "traveled" farther in life than you. Read books, listen to tapes, and keep your eyes and ears open. Turn off the TV and open your mind. Both of you are very bright and have tremendous potential.

When you meet new people, learn from them. I've never met a person I couldn't learn something from—even if it's learning what I don't want to be like. I met a shoeshine man in the Dallas airport, and he began to tell me about his family. I could tell by his words and the way he spoke that he was well educated. He was a kind man, and a good and loving grandfather. He had retired, but wanted his grandkids to be the first in his family to go to college, so he was working to help pay their tuition. Before he retired, he was an elementary teacher, but he was too old to teach and couldn't find a job anywhere. I learned from him that love, and desire for legacy, is powerful enough to overcome pride. I learned from him that sacrifice for a loved one creates deep and fulfilling joy. I thought about what he did and realized I would be willing to work anywhere necessary if I could benefit your future.

If you stop learning, you stop growing, and if you stop growing—well, you just stop.

Apply what you learn. Learning is not for learning's sake. Gaining knowledge just to know things is not the point. Learning must change our lives or it has little value. To change our lives, knowledge must be applied to everyday living. For example, you could take karate lessons from the best teacher east of the Mississippi, but if you don't practice, the lessons will do you no good. Some things work and some things don't, but we keep learning, applying, changing, and growing.

Share what you learn with others. That is the best part. For years I've had dozens and dozens of cassette tapes, and after I listen to them and file the notes, the tapes just sit in a file drawer or cabinet and gather dust. That's dumb! I have begun sending each tape after I've finished with it to one of the Joshua's Men (Joshua's Men are the guys in my leadership development group) with a little note of encouragement attached. It's fun! I read articles, magazines, and journals on the plane when I travel. I love tearing out articles that will become lessons to help pastors and churches become healthy and grow. Sometimes I find articles, quotes, and ideas in books about raising kids, and I bring them home to Mom, so we can learn to be better parents.

Most of all, I love learning and passing things on to you, such as these letters. I hope these thoughts find a place in your heart, and you pass some of them on to your kids and others you love.

Still learning . . .

Dad

Finishing Well | Dr. John C. Maxwell

Founder of INJOY, Inc.; Atlanta, Georgia
Written to his two children, Elizabeth and Joel-Porter

Dear Elizabeth and Joel-Porter,

I'm fifty-one years old. If my life were divided into twelve monthly segments I would be in August. It goes so fast. I can remember as if it were yesterday bringing you kids home for the first time. That was unquestionably one of the greatest gifts and privileges of my life. I have learned as I grow older—watch it, I'm not that old!—that beginnings are brief and are largely out of our control, but how we finish is completely up to us.

Finishing well is one of life's greatest challenges and privileges. Mother Teresa went to be with the Lord not long ago. The godly woman gave her life to others. She gave her life to the poorest of the poor in Calcutta, India. Joel, you were blessed to have traveled to Calcutta and to have seen firsthand the powerful ministry of Mother Teresa. Your most prized possession is a picture of you two standing together at her place of ministry. As you know, she founded the Missionaries of Charity and touched thousands of lives. She finished well. Billy Graham is still with us, but is losing his physical stamina. Nonetheless, he continues to preach and tell the world about Jesus. Through all the decades his moral character has never been in question, never once. There is no doubt when the Lord chooses to take him home, he will have finished well.

Mother Teresa and Billy Graham are celebrated people in history. Elizabeth and Joel, you are celebrated people in my heart. But lest it seem too great a gap, let me tell you about someone close to all of us in the Maxwell family. Grampa Maxwell. My dad, your grampa, is my hero. All his life he has been faithful to God, his family, and people he has served in Christian ministry. Two years ago when Dad had a heart attack, it scared us all. Those tense days in the hospital reminded us of how important family is and how important it is to love one another to the fullest. It reminded us of how much Grampa Maxwell has invested in our lives. I will never forget the afternoon in the hospital when he laid hands on both of you and asked God to cover your lives with grace and blessing. Kids, God has numbered our days, and we must choose to live each one to the fullest. Grampa Maxwell will finish well—very well. You know how he has lived his life. You have watched the pageant of his days unfold as you grew up. To this day he continues to love, give, and invest in others. I can think of no better vision to cast for you in this idea of finishing well.

In contrast, I think of a few of my pastor friends who started so well, but finished so poorly. The loss is devastating, the price is high, and the regret runs deep.

Finishing well begins today. You can't wait until the end of your life to begin finishing well. Life is a process. Finishing well begins every day when you get up in the

Finishing well begins every day
when you get up in the morning.

morning. You've teased me about dieting over the years. I always want to start tomorrow, and that obviously doesn't work!

Finishing well involves making good decisions on a daily basis. I'm so proud of both of you. I've watched you grow up and learn to make good decisions, sometimes by making poor ones, but you've learned! At age fifty-one, I have learned that this process never ends. We continually learn to make wise decisions and, more important, live our lives by those decisions. Elizabeth, when I officiated at your wedding last year, I was privileged to give you away as a father and bless your marriage as a minister. Your mother and I pray every day that you and Steve will always make your decisions in harmony with God and each other.

Finishing well calls for being faithful to our commitments and convictions. It was one thing for me to decide to marry your mother nearly thirty years ago (a wise choice, I would add); it's quite another to live out on a daily basis the commitments of a faithful and loving husband. You have watched me live out my commitments and convictions as you've grown up, and I trust my example is an encouragement to you in how to finish well.

Finishing well means giving more than receiving. This I believe with all my heart. Your mother and I have committed our lives to giving to others. The irony is that God has given us so much more than we could have ever expected. My joy has been to give to you, and I delight in seeing you give to others. Many things come to mind, in particular, one of our family Christmas traditions of giving gifts to needy and less privileged families. My heart is warmed in my memories of your joy as we gave. I know you will continue to be givers.

Finishing well means closing out this life with a victorious Christian testimony. After Grampa Maxwell's heart attack, he wrote an open letter in a magazine to many people who have known him over the years. I have not yet shared his words with you. Let me share the letter with you now:

God has been so good to me to trust me to preach the gospel for more than half a century. It has been a heavenly privilege to serve Him in the various ways He has directed through these years.

For the past ten years the Lord has helped me to glorify Him in evangelistic meetings. On May 8th, after completing three blessed revivals in South Carolina and arriving home by plane, the next morning about 3:00 a.m., I awoke with an unusual chest pain.

Later I was taken to Winter Haven Hospital and then transferred to Florida Hospital in Orlando, Florida. The diagnosis was a major heart attack with a completely closed artery, leaving 1/3 of my heart dead. While in Florida Hospital I had a repeated attack. I was anointed and felt assured I would be returning home. When I told the good nurse I was going home, she replied, "You mean to heaven?" I answered with assurance, "To Winter Haven," where I am now recovering.

However, since my evangelism does require much travel and weeks away from home, I have canceled all revivals and camps this year. Since the fire still burns within me, my ministry will change; but I will be busy in special ministries as God directs.

It is with high regard, overflowing love and sincere appreciation to all our ministers and laymen who have prayed for me and supported my ministry that all blessings and achievements are direct from God. For it all we give God all the praise, but are not forgetful of all those who have been a part of my ministry and fellow-laborers together with me.

We all do have the inward assurance that His rewards far exceed our labors. His grace is inexpressible, the cause of Christ is immeasurable, and the future is incomprehensible. "Yes, I feel like traveling on."

In His Love,
Melvin Maxwell

My prayer is that someday, all of us in the Maxwell family will be able to leave this world with such a clear testimony of our walk with God.

I love you both very much,
Dad

Risk | Dan Reiland

Dear John-Peter,

We were 12,500 feet above ground and about to take a huge risk. Your mom and I were prepared to jump out of a perfectly good airplane and skydive for the very first time.

Ground school was limited. They taught us three basic things. The good news was that there were only three; the bad news was that there was no margin for error. All three must be accomplished successfully for a safe landing. The first thing was to form a proper arch with our bodies as we left the plane. If we didn't accomplish this correctly, we could begin to unintentionally tumble, which for beginners is bad news. We could end up with our arms tangled in the cables to the canopy. Not a good thing. Second, they taught us about pulling the rip cord. A bright orange handle was the connection to our lifeline. It was to be pulled at 5,000 feet. We were

instructed to watch the altimeter on our wrists to know when it was time. Last was the flare. That was about pulling the cables to flare the canopy for a soft and graceful landing. Well, at least a landing that wouldn't break your ankles or some other part of your body!

It was time to jump. For our first jump the instructor was literally attached to us. You never know who will lose it on the first try. My instructor launched us out the door and yelled, "Who's your best friend?" I screamed with conviction, "You are!" The arch was good! We were speeding toward the earth in excess of one hundred miles an hour. My cheeks were flapping, my heart was pounding, and in that moment I realized I might have been wise to wear plastic pants.

I missed the 5,000-foot marker to pull the bright orange handle, and a second or so later I was at 3,500 feet! The instructor slapped my leg to either see if I was still conscious or remind me to pull the cord before we both ended up like the Coyote on a Roadrunner cartoon. I pulled the cord, and we went from over one hundred miles an hour to maybe twenty-five miles an hour in two seconds. My underwear found a new place to call home.

The flare was easy, and we glided in for a not so graceful, but nonetheless soft landing. Success! We've all enjoyed the video of this event, but more important is what I learned.

Risk is the gateway to the best things in life, perhaps to life itself. For the first time in my life I understood the true meaning of no plan B. There was no changing my mind and no going back. I never felt more alive.

Fear prevents risk. Several of our friends said they would never do such a thing as jump from an airplane. I will give them credit for perhaps possessing more wisdom than those of us who jumped, but I know what they missed. The important thing is not to allow fear to prevent you from living all that life has to offer you.

My friend Dave Marlow took a risk when he started his own electronic printing business. It scared him half to death, but he knew he must try. He didn't want to work for someone else the

Risk is the gateway to the best things in life, perhaps to life itself.

rest of his life and wonder what it would have been like to own a business and work for himself. Dave is doing marvelously well.

I remember one of your first risks in life. It was the first time you dived headfirst into the deep end of a swimming pool. You were just as scared as Dave was, but you jumped. In that instant a whole new window to the world opened to you: the joy of swimming and playing in a pool.

I remember the risk I took when I asked your mom to marry me. My knees were knocking, my heart was pounding, and I could hardly form a word on my lips. My mouth felt as if it were filled with saltine crackers and the Spackle carpenters use on drywall. She was so beautiful, and I was, well, I was not! What would she say? What if she said no? What would her dad say? What if he said, "You've got to be kidding!"? I asked her and she said yes! (And Pop gave his blessing too.)

Older people tell me that one of their top regrets in life was not taking enough risks.

Taking risks is what life is about. Avoiding risks is missing out on life. Caution may keep us safe, but safe isn't living.

There are some risks that don't make sense—crossing a street without looking both ways or driving without a seat belt, for example. Cheating is a risk that doesn't make sense. Giving all your money to a complete stranger who promises he will double it for you is a foolish risk. Loaning your car to someone without a license or insurance is not a sensible risk. Common sense will cover things like these, and as you think about these examples, none of them add value to life. They are corner-cutting risks, the kind that steal from life, not add to it.

Too many people live their whole lives without living at all. Take a risk. Talk to a stranger. Try a new food. Go back to school. Tell your boss what you think. Put some money in a long-shot stock. Tell your neighbor about Jesus. Write a candid, heartfelt letter to a friend, sharing how you really feel. Say no to the government by voting your convictions or getting involved in local politics. Move to a new city. Quit your job and start fresh; do what you want to do.

Risk without wisdom is not what I mean. You must do your homework. Look for three things, and if you find them, go for it! First, seek God's blessing. Second, think it through clearly. Third, feel a passion in your heart that puts a knot in your stomach. If you get these green lights, it's time to jump!

Love,
Dad

Don't worry that your children
never listen to you;
worry that they are always watching you.

Robert Fulghum

Consistency | Zig Ziglar

Author and Speaker, Chairman—Zig Ziglar Corporation; Dallas, Texas
Written to his four children and four grandchildren

Dear kids,

I have something important to say to you, and I start with a parable from an unknown author. It seems that fire, water, and trust were headed for a dense forest. Fearing they might become separated in the heavy foliage, they discussed ways in which they might be reunited. Fire stated, "It will be easy—just look for smoke because where you see smoke, you will know I am close by." Water said, "Just look for a lush, green meadow and you will know I'm there." Trust said, "I suggest you not lose sight of me because once I am lost, it is very difficult to find me again."

The message is clear. Think about it. All successful personal and business relationships that endure are built on trust. Husband-wife, parent-child, brother-sister, employer-employee, salesperson-customer relationships are all built on trust, and once that trust is betrayed, it is very difficult to recapture. Many times it takes years, and sometimes trust is never completely regained.

Your relationships with God, family, friends, and associates play a major role in your health, happiness, prosperity, security, peace of mind, and hope for your future. Fortunately, God is a forgiving God who, when asked, will forgive even denial and betrayal. That is seldom true with man.

It's safe to say that the biggest failures in life are results of character flaws, not lack of ability. The media daily carry stories of celebrities, politicians, athletes, businesspeople, and even men and women of the cloth who "had it all" until character flaws destroyed them.

The question is, How do we gain and

maintain trust? The answer is consistency. The type of person we portray ourselves to be should never deviate from the core person we are. I'm speaking about character and integrity, the parents of trust.

Consistency of words and actions is critical. In my lifetime I have seen some tragedies that resulted from a loss of trust. Early in my career two men whom I trusted and respected turned out to have feet of clay. What they appeared to be in public was a far cry from what they were in private. To be honest, finding out the truth about them broke my heart, and yet at the same time it had a very positive

impact on my life. As a result of my experience with them, I determined that if I ever reached any level of prominence where people looked to me for guidance in any area, I would work hard to maintain consistency in everything I did and said.

The tragedy of inconsistency is evidenced in a statement made by Mahatma Gandhi: "I would have become a Christian, had it not been for Christians." With simple eloquence he was saying that many people who professed Christianity obviously did not possess Christ. The Lord would call them hypocrites, and He had some particularly unkind things to say

All successful personal and business
relationships that endure are built on trust.

about them throughout the Scriptures. I frequently tell little funnies about hypocrites when I describe a hypocrite as an individual who gripes and complains about the sex, nudity, and violence on his VCR, and I mention that a hypocrite is also a person who is not himself on Sunday.

People laugh when I say those things, but it's not a laughing matter. It's deadly serious and tragic in many ways.

Inconsistency in marriage when the faithfulness pledge is broken frequently leads to divorce, always leads to heartbreak, and many times leads to abandonment, poverty, and dysfunctional families. Having someone in the workplace who is one way when face-to-face with you and completely different behind your back leads to conflict, tension, and lower productivity. Attending church on Sunday for a little "halo adjustment" and then embezzling from the company lead to bankruptcy, possible incarceration, loss of job and respect, and destruction of the families involved.

With a consistent life you don't have to spend time thinking about what you've said or done because each decision you make is based on maintaining your integrity, which is a hallmark of consistency. With integrity you do the right thing, which eliminates guilt. With integrity you have nothing to fear because you have nothing to hide, and when you remove guilt and fear from your life, your pathway to the top is easier and faster.

I encourage you, kids, to look at your family. Each of you has said to your mom and me that you never doubted that Mom and Dad loved you and that we loved each other. That consistency gave all of you a sense of stability. We worked to combine this with a consistency in our relationships with each of you as we made our decisions. If something was illegal or immoral, it was not open for discussion; everything else was negotiable, so long as it did not endanger your health or reputation.

I hope the message is clear, and one that you will take seriously. Consistency of words and actions in your personal, family, and business lives will give you the best chance to enjoy more of the things money will buy and all of the things money won't buy. Consistency of effort in whatever you do will guarantee respect from your fellowman and will ensure success in your career. Consistency in worshiping our Lord will lead to a happier life and guarantee your place in eternity with Him, which you secured long ago by accepting Him as your Lord and Savior. I encourage you to continue to look to Him as your role model in everything because Jesus Christ is the same yesterday, today, and forever. That's consistency.

Fortunately, consistency does not depend entirely on you. When you really know your arithmetic, you can live in a godly manner that will please our Lord. Just remember that you plus God equals *enough*.

I love you,
Dad

Never Surrender Your Freedom | Dan Reiland

Dear Mackenzie and John-Peter,
Grandpa Diaz was in the navy for more than twenty years. Pop was at sea on those big gray battleships for many months at a time. He could have chosen a career that enabled him to be at home more to enjoy some of his favorite pastimes, but he gave up that freedom and chose to serve and protect his country. Pop and many others worked to provide for us one of life's most precious gifts—freedom. I want you to understand, cherish, and never surrender this freedom.

Let me begin by saying that this idea of freedom does not include simply "doing your own thing." It doesn't mean doing whatever you want. The freedom I'm talking about is the freedom to do whatever you want as long as it doesn't hurt anyone else or rob others of their freedom. Even better, it's a freedom that actually benefits you *and* others.

When I was growing up in the sixties and early seventies, thousands of young people were unhappy with the government and took a stand against war in general and the Vietnam War in particular. They were called hippies or flower children. They had long hair, sang songs about peace and love, and marched against war. I know it's hard for you to imagine your daddy with long hair. Actually, it's hard for you to imagine me with any hair! I'll show you pictures sometime. I liked the music (still do!), and at that time I, too, saw war as senseless. I still find war cruel and sad, but I have since grown to understand that there are some things worth fighting for. The hippies wanted freedom—that was good—but they went about it in a way that didn't benefit anyone, including themselves. Many turned to drugs and forfeited the very thing they stood for— freedom to think, freedom to act responsibly, and even freedom to live. (Some took so many drugs, they overdosed and died.) My point is that you can go about your freedom in a right way and a wrong way.

As a teenager, I wanted long hair, and my mom, your grammy, wanted it short. I wanted my freedom to have it the way I wanted. I remember saying to her, "You're not the boss of my life." I also wanted freedom to avoid my homework, skip some chores, and stay out late at night. She helped me understand that wasn't freedom at all, but I was a prisoner to my selfishness. It was a good lesson. Had I not learned it, my life would have turned out much differently. Many of my friends who "rebelled" never learned how

to gain freedom with responsibility, and to this day they have trouble keeping jobs and making their marriages last.

It may seem that I'm writing more about surrendering your freedom than not surrendering it. You must first understand the right kind of freedom before you set your sights on holding on to it. Keep reading!

Never sacrifice your freedom to think and express your thoughts for fear of not being accepted. You will be tempted to live against your convictions, the things you really believe in, or perhaps just be silent because of what others might think. Don't. Speak up! Stand up! Be heard! You will be tempted at times to

The best freedom is the freedom to give, love, serve, and make a difference in people's lives.

try to be someone other than yourself to fit in with the crowd. Don't. Be yourself at all times. This is the right kind of freedom.

Never sacrifice your freedom to do what you want for money. Someday you will have a job, and your boss may ask you to do some things you don't believe in or you know in your heart are wrong. Don't do them, and certainly don't do them just to receive your paycheck. Your freedom is more valuable than the biggest paycheck you can ever imagine. Even if you lose your job, you will keep something far more important—the freedom to be true to yourself.

Never sacrifice your freedom to learn and grow so that you can keep your friends happy. Your friends are responsible for their own happiness. There will come a day when some of your friends will want to play and party and will want you to go with them, but you'll know you need to study or do something that helps you continue to grow and learn. Don't surrender! Your friends will be there for another day, and if they are truly your friends,

they will understand and want the best for you.

The best freedom is the freedom to give, love, serve, and make a difference in people's lives. The greatest freedom of all is freedom from the penalty of sin. This gift is provided for you by Jesus. His death on the cross paid the price for your sin. Your faith and belief in Jesus Christ give you the capacity to live, not perfectly, but forgiven. They give you the freedom to be the wonderful creation God designed you to be. The apostle Paul told us, "Stand fast therefore in the liberty by which Christ has made us free [free from a life of sinful behavior and ultimately free from the penalty of sinful behavior]" (Gal. 5:1). He also said, "You, brethren, have been called to [freedom]; only do not use [freedom] as an opportunity for the flesh, but through love serve one another" (Gal. 5:13).

With this in mind, my dear children, live free!

Love,

Dad

Sexual Purity | Josh McDowell

Author and Speaker; Director of the Josh McDowell Ministry; Dallas, Texas
Campus Crusade for Christ, International
Written to his children, Kelly and Sean

Dear Kelly and Sean,

You both know I've crisscrossed the United States for the past couple of years speaking, appearing on radio and TV shows, and talking to young people about their sexuality. You've been with me on some of those trips.

Tears have filled my eyes more times than I can remember as I have listened to personal stories guys and girls have told me. My heart has been broken as they have talked about how their lives have been messed up because they didn't understand or know how to manage their sexuality.

If there was ever a gift your mom and I want you, Kelly, and you, Sean, to have, besides spiritual life itself, it's the gift of sexual wholeness. It can be yours if you make it through the world's minefield of teen sexual pressure with-

out getting blown up emotionally.

Do you remember a while back when we all spent a day together at the San Diego Zoo? (Who could ever forget the face that baboon made at you, Sean?) We had a great day, didn't we? And one of the things that helped make it great was something that's usually thought of as being very restrictive—all those black bars on the cages and the big fences around the animal compounds.

There were moments when we thought we could have gotten a much better look by going past the barriers. But you know that if we had, it would have been terror rather than more fun. The barriers were there to protect us from the animals and provide for our safety.

And truthfully, that's exactly why God put up some barriers in our lives. Sex is one

39

Because I love you so much,
I would like to see you make good choices
and avoid mistakes if you can.

area in which there are barriers that you are becoming aware of. God's rules on sex are there to protect us from getting emotionally wounded and to provide for the maximum pleasure of our sexuality as we follow His guidelines. People do enter those cages and compounds at the zoo, but only after they've been trained in how to do so safely. Those people discover a thrill in working with those animals that we can't know just looking in from the outside.

That's a lot like the way it is with sex. When you understand God's purpose for it and enter its "compound" in God's timing, the experience that follows can be thrilling.

Kelly, I see you as a woman who knows how to enjoy her beauty and her female feelings to the maximum. But it must be in ways that do not lure and trap guys into wanting to take advantage of you. I picture you saving yourself and your gift of sex for one special guy. He is growing up somewhere in the world right now. He is the guy who will capture your heart and give you the kind of genuine love God has planned for you.

Sean, in my mind's eye I see you becoming a man who is as handsome and healthy as they come. I see you as a person who enjoys his physical strength and ability. And I picture you being mature and secure enough to brush aside the pressures to be "experienced" before marriage. I see you knowing how to have fun and entertain the girls you date without pressuring them to share their physical affections with you.

I see you doing this because you have discovered for yourself the genuine power of God's Holy Spirit, a force in your life that makes wanting to please God more important to you than pleasing me or Mom or even your closest friends. And, Sean, I promise that to the best of my ability, I'll always model this kind of man for you.

Kelly and Sean, as your dad, I want both of you to know that mere words can never express the intensity of the love I feel for you. I know someday, Sean, you'll understand just how deeply a father can feel love for his son or daughter. And Kelly, you'll know the unbelievable strength of a mother's love.

Next to my love for God and your mother, I love the two of you and your sisters, Katie and Heather, more than life itself.

I've told you many times that no mistake

you could ever make in life could cause me to stop loving you. And it's true because God's love is at the foundation of my love for each of you. The Bible is very clear that "in this is love, not that we loved God, but that He loved us and sent His Son to be the propitiation for our sins" (1 John 4:10). And just as you can't turn off God's love, there is no stopping mine either, no matter what mistake or choice you will ever make. But because I love you so much, I would like to see you make good choices and avoid mistakes if you can.

With both of you, Kelly and Sean, I've always had the honor of your trust and open communication. I realize that's probably going to be tested many times in the next few years as you become more your own adult selves. But in that process I want you to know something very, very important. There will never be anything you think about that I won't be interested in listening to you say. There will never be any question you can even imagine asking that I won't want to hear.

And that's not because I feel I have to know everything about you. It's because, after God and your mom, you are the best friends I have in this world. I want to talk and laugh and cry and struggle and serve and win with you for the rest of my life.

Well, dear Kelly and Sean, here is my letter to you. Wow! Do I ever love you both!

Dad

Before You Say, "I Do" | Dan Reiland

Dear Mackenzie and John-Peter,

Let me tell you my favorite love story. The first time I saw your mom my heart jumped. I was in the college group at church, and I wondered if a creature as beautiful as this one named Patti could ever be interested in me. Well, she was! On one of our first dates we were having lunch at Old Town in San Diego. I don't know if it was her smile, the way the sun played off her hair, or the confident sparkle in her eyes, but I knew she was gorgeous, and I loved being with her. I remember the first time I knew I loved your mom. We were praying for someone and tears welled up in her eyes. I saw her heart and knew it was wonderful. She cared about people, and that is so important. The first time we kissed, I thought my stomach would come up through my nose, and the tingle went down to my toes. That was in 1978, and we married in 1981, nearly eighteen years ago. It gets better every year.

You can have a wonderful marriage too. Since before you were born, I have been praying that each of you would marry a wonderful Christian. This is the most important thing to remember before you say, "I do." No amount of love will make up for the gap that will exist between you and your spouse if you marry someone who doesn't love God. In addition, there are several other things to keep in mind.

Before you say, "I do," make sure you enjoy conversation with each other. Communication is the heart of your relationship. If you can't talk, plain talk, before you get married, you won't magically be able to after you get married. Talking for hours on end must be something fun and exciting for you. Conversation is the way you discover each other for the rest of your lives. Continual discovery keeps the marriage alive.

Before you say, "I do," make sure you

would be willing to be together without all the kissing and hugging. Don't misunderstand, kissing is great! Lots of kissing is even better! But the relationship must not be based on the physical. Your relationship must be based on the heart.

Before you say, "I do," make sure you are willing to make a sacrificial life commitment to your future spouse. Getting married isn't about *marrying* just the right person as much as it is *becoming* just the right person. Getting married isn't the way to get all your needs met; it's the way in which you attempt to meet someone else's needs. If you don't love someone enough to serve him or her, don't get married. Your mom isn't thrilled about washing my underwear. She says, "Those things could walk by themselves!" But she does anyway. That's sacrificial servanthood.

Before you say, "I do," recognize that no marriage is easy or perfect. It takes work and dedication to enjoy a healthy marriage relationship. Your mom and I have some disagreements, but we always love each other. We are committed to each other, no matter what.

My heart is warmed as I look forward to two very special days in my life and yours. These are the days when each of you walks the aisle with your chosen life mate. Just to be your dad will be my great joy. Knowing you made the right choice will be your great joy. I'll be proud of you for choosing well.

I love you,

Dad

Since before you were born, I have been praying that each of you would marry a wonderful Christian.

Money, Marriage, and Life with God | Dr. Kenneth N. Taylor

Special Consultant, New Living Translation, Tyndale House Publishers; Wheaton, Illinois

Written to his twenty-eight grandchildren

Dear kids,

I love each one of you, and I long for you to live a happy and contented life and, as I have said to some of you personally, for you to be a joy to God and mankind alike.

Here in this letter I will tell you about some good things I have done and recommend to you; and some things I didn't do, but want you to do.

Begin now to put aside 10 percent of all you earn, and invest the money in mutual funds in the stock market. Why? Because in God's providence the value of the average share of stock has grown 10 percent a year for the past fifty years. A $1,500 investment this year doubles to become $3,000 seven years from now. Fourteen years from now the $3,000 will have become $6,000, and so on,

doubling every seven years. So by the fiftieth year that $1,500 becomes worth $200,000. The same thing happens to the $1,500 you invest next year. By the time you are sixty-five years old, having regularly invested 10 percent of your income, you will be a multimillionaire. Meanwhile, inflation and cost of living will also grow astronomically, but at only a third as much as your stock market growth.

Now, what to do with that money: use what you need for retirement expenses, and give the rest to God. Retirement years look so far away to you now that you can't even dream that such a time exists. Trust me when I say those years are there awaiting you, and when you get there and you look back to this year, it will seem very short.

With a fortune at your disposal, it will be

I long for you to live a happy and contented life and for you to be a joy to God and mankind alike.

a pleasure to give gifts to aid your church and the work of God in various parts of the world and in various ways. Aid to poor people pleases God immensely. Help those who are hungry to eat. Some organizations give small loans to those who can't borrow at ruinous rates from money lenders. There are ways to help people buy Bibles and ways to help nationals start churches that will reach hundreds and thousands with the message of God.

Begin to give weekly or monthly to God's work. I think a tithe (10 percent) is a good place to begin. The Bible doesn't say 10 percent, but it says to give regularly, based on your income for the week. Grandma and I were taught this tithing principle as children, and we have carried it out faithfully through thick and thin—sometimes very thin. Now we can give more. We believe there is reward in heaven for people who give faithfully as well as a lot of satisfaction now in giving to good causes. We believe God sees, and is pleased, and cares for the needs of those who honor and thank Him with their weekly or regular giving.

The second topic I want to discuss with you is marriage. Most of you will marry. Fridays are currently the days I pray for each of the twenty-eight of you by name and situation. One of the things I pray urgently about is that if marriage is in God's plan for you, you will find a life partner who will trust and serve God with you, and together you will bring up your children for the glory of God, as boys and girls of fairness and fun, to grow to be men and women of God.

I also pray for those who in the will of God won't marry. That will be tough. God has given almost everyone a desire for marriage and love and sex and children, and to be deprived of these seems unfair. But I believe God will somehow compensate. To rush into a marriage in order to be married is dangerous and probably wrong. To marry a person who is not a follower of Christ is wrong if you belong to God. To marry a person who says, "I follow the Lord," but isn't in tune with God is, I believe, equally dangerous and wrong. It's better to remain unmarried than to have a life of disagreement over these basic matters. Who is running your life and deciding about marriage—you or God?

I repeat part of that question for all of you: Who is running your life—you or God? How much I have prayed for each of you, and will continue to do so, that you will ask God to take your life and use it. And that you will turn away from all evil. Follow Christ in all you do. Commit your life to Him. It will make all the difference in the world now and in the life to come.

Perhaps you already know my hope that you will have a regular daily time of Bible reading and a time of prayer. You experience cleansing and strength from the Holy Spirit through the writings from God, and great power in trusting prayer. I pray that this will be true for you.

Don't go it alone. Be a regular attender of a church. A stick burning alone only smolders. When joined with others, it bursts into flame. You help them and they help you. Please consider this an imperative for growth in grace.

With very much love,

Grandpa

The righteous man walks
in his integrity;
His children are blessed after him.

Proverbs 20:7

Y

Live on Purpose | Dan Reiland

Dear Mackenzie and John-Peter,
You have always enjoyed pinball machines.
There is something fun about a chance game
where you pull the lever and the ball is flung
out of a chute and bounced around at random
without any choice of its own direction as it
collides into various bumpers, springs, and
paddles. The whole time whistles are going
off, buzzers are ringing, and the machine gives
you thousands of points! Your favorite part
was just before the little silver ball's wild ride
was over, you got to take a swing at it with

those two little bats controlled from the but-
tons on the outside. When you swung at the
ball and hit it, it flew at high speed right back
into the chaos of bumpers and whistles for
another wild and random ride.

My observation in life is that many people
live by the pinball principle. Each morning they
get up, and without an intentional focus or purpose, they are flung into the day's activities and
responsibilities because someone else has pulled
their "lever." Someone else who *is* living on purpose. Throughout the day, they bounce around

at random, and on occasion, just when they think they will slide into their own spot, the "swat" of someone else's agenda sends them flailing back into the noisy chaos of endless activity without a sense of purpose. By the end of the day they are so tired, they just line up to be catapulted back into the same thing the next day and the next and the next. Soon a lifetime has gone by. They put a few points on the board, but they really didn't add up to anything.

My dear children, you must live your life with passion, on purpose, by intention. You must live deliberately. Listen to these powerful words by George Bernard Shaw. They resonate deeply within me and I want to pass them on to you:

This is the true joy in life—being used for a purpose recognized by yourself as a mighty one, being a force of nature instead of a feverish, selfish little clod of ailments and grievances, complaining that the world will not devote itself to making you happy. I am of the opinion that my life belongs to the whole community as long as I live, it is my privilege to do for it whatever I can. I want to be thoroughly used up when I die, for the harder I work, the more I live. I rejoice in life for its own sake. Life is no brief candle to me. It is sort of a splendid torch which I've got a hold of for the moment, and I want to make it burn as brightly as possible before handing it on to future generations.

My dear children, you must live your life with passion, on purpose, by intention.

In his book *Who Switched the Price Tags?* Anthony Campolo related the words of the pastor of a black Baptist church, speaking to a group of college students in his congregation:

"Children," he said, "you're going to die! . . . One of these days, they're going to take you out to the cemetery, drop you in a hole, throw some dirt on your face, and go back to the church and eat potato salad.

"When you were born," he said, "you alone were crying and everybody else was happy. The important questions I want you to ask are these: When you die are you alone going to be happy, leaving everybody else crying? The answer depends on whether you live to get titles or you live to get testimonies. When they lay you in the grave, are people going to stand around reciting the fancy titles you earned, or are they going to stand around giving testimonies of the good things you did for them? . . .

*"Will you leave behind just a newspaper column telling people how important you were, or will you leave crying people who give testi-*monies of how they've lost the best friend they've ever had?"*

God has designed you for a special purpose, a mission, that you intentionally and deliberately live out. We are all called to love God and serve man, and that is a noble cause. But it's generic; it's for everyone. God created you with a specific plan in mind.

[Paul said,] "I may finish my race with joy, and the ministry which I received from the Lord Jesus." (Acts 20:24)

We are His workmanship, created in Christ Jesus for good works, which God prepared beforehand that we should walk in them. (Eph. 2:10)

Do not be unwise, but understand what the will of the Lord is. (Eph. 5:17).

Find what brings you joy and fulfillment, and do it to your fullest. Do it on purpose with all the passion of your heart, soul, and mind. Do it as unto the Lord to bring Him glory and honor. If you don't run your life, someone else will. You have only one life to live—live it on purpose. Don't let the years speed by and end up sitting in a rocking chair staring at a gold watch and wondering, "Was this all life was about?"

Eric Hoffer offered these wise words: "The feeling of being hurried is not usually the result of living a full life and having no time. It is, on the contrary, born of a vague fear that we are wasting our life. When we do not do the one thing we ought to do, we have no time for anything else—we are the busiest people in the world."

You liked that movie *City Slickers* with Billy Crystal. Remember when Curly was riding on his horse and said that we need to find the "one thing" we are supposed to do, and not worry about anything else? That's the idea! You must find this one thing on your own. My passion is that you discover what it is and live richly, deeply, and deliberately.

Love,

Dad

The Love of God | Dr. Larry Crabb

Founder, Institute for Biblical Community; Morrison, Colorado, Psychologist, Author, and Delighted Grandfather
Written to his granddaughter, Josie

Dear Josie,

Somewhere, in the very center of who you really are, right now, at six months old, you are experiencing the most powerful and wonderful force in the world.

I first met you when you were four days old. You were feeling it then as your mother held you. You couldn't see your mother very clearly as you rested in her arms, but I could. Not just her arms, but also her eyes were embracing you. Everything that makes her a mother was showing through those beautiful dark eyes and wrapping itself like a snug blanket around you.

On the day of your birth, a new mother was born. A new way came into being for Jesus to speak His love to a little girl He had already created in His mind, a long time ago.

The most powerful and wonderful force in the world was pouring out of your mother's heart into yours.

You were feeling it as your daddy brought his face close to yours and whispered your name. You came into this world a sick little girl. Your daddy would have done anything—anything!—to make you well. You weren't aware of it then, but because he was there, you were protected by a greater strength than yours that would stop at nothing to help you. You felt safe as you heard your name through your daddy's lips. The most powerful and wonderful force in the world was carried into you by that whisper.

Josie, you are now a half-year old. I am 106 half-years old. Let me tell you what I've learned: *the most powerful and wonderful force in the world is enough to get you through what-ever your life will bring.* Cling to it! Believe in it! Trust it!

I'm writing this to you during the most difficult season of my life, all 106 half-years. I was very ill this past summer, and I might be sick again. Some people I love are going through hard times that I can't fix. I'm afraid, my heart is heavy, and sometimes I cry.

The dam burst this morning. All the terrible feelings that I try so hard not to feel stormed through me like a flash flood.

I called a friend. He gave me an experience of the most powerful and wonderful force in the world. When I called him, I could

barely speak. After we talked, I couldn't help singing. I sang "It Is Well with My Soul." I had to—and I meant it.

Josie, that's a miracle, a miracle I want you to taste time and time again. I don't want you to go through hard times, but you will. It's just the way life is. I'd gladly give my life if I knew it would guarantee your happiness. But Someone has already done that!

And that same Someone has made the most powerful and wonderful force in the world available to you; no, more than that, He has filled a big bucket with it and poured it all over you; no, more than that, He has found a way to pour it in you so it's always there for you to depend on.

The most powerful and wonderful force in the world is enough to get you through whatever your life will bring.

I hope you read this letter when you're eight years old and your best friend has decided she likes someone else better. I hope you read this letter when you're twelve and a boy you're noticing isn't noticing you.

I hope you read this letter when you're sixteen and you've just performed poorly in something that really mattered to you. I hope you read this letter when you're nineteen and you've done something wrong that you feel you can't tell anyone, especially your parents.

I hope you read this letter when you're twenty-six and a big dream, a really big one, has just been shattered and you're wondering whether life is worth living. I hope you read this letter when you're thirty-seven and everything feels just too much to handle.

I hope you read this letter when you're forty-two and someone you deeply love has just died. I hope you read this letter when you're fifty-three (106 half-years old) and you feel so scared and sad that you cry as you've never cried before.

I hope you read this letter when you're sixty-eight and sick and feeling lonely. I hope you read this letter when you're eighty-two and wonder whether anyone cares.

Josie, at every moment of your life, in all the good times—and you'll have many—as well as the bad times, the most powerful and wonderful force in all the world will be in you if you know Jesus. It will get you through the worst of times and help you celebrate the best of times with abandon. It will give you hope and even joy, not always right away, not always soon, but always eventually, and when it comes, the hope will be overflowing and the joy unspeakable.

Josie, remember, when life looks hopelessly dark and joylessly awful, you're not living in the last chapter of your story. Look ahead. Read how it all ends. The climax reveals the most powerful and wonderful force in the world, and it helps you believe it's at work right now.

To you, Josie, I'm an old man. Let me sit back in my rocking chair, sip my coffee, think over my life, then sit up, look you gently in the eye, and say with all the passion in my heart that loves you so much: "God looks at you and He bursts into song." He is hopelessly in love with you. He is actually as excited about loving you as He is about loving Jesus. Nothing you ever do will make Him love you more; He can't. And nothing you ever do will make Him love you less; He can't do that either.

The love of God is the most powerful and wonderful force in the world. It's stronger than every rejection, every failure, every tragedy, every worry, every hurt. It comes to Grandmother Vicki and Granddad Tim. It comes to you through your mother and dad in ways only they can give. But most of all, it comes to you through Jesus, and through Him, it always comes perfectly.

Whatever goes right, you are loved. Whatever goes wrong, our hearts still sing with love, maybe a little louder then because it's harder to hear when life isn't going so well. Josie, my beloved granddaughter, follow the path that will take you into your heavenly Father's arms. You're already in His heart.

With passion beyond words, I give you to Jesus. He is the most powerful and wonderful force in the world.

Love,
Grandpa

Honesty | Dan Reiland

Dear Mackenzie and John-Peter,

According to an old story, someone cut down a cherry tree! Mr. Washington went to his son, George, and asked him if he did it. Young George Washington said, "I cannot tell a lie. I cut down the cherry tree." I think George could have told a lie! The important lesson to learn here is that he chose not to. He chose to be honest.

I was amazed when the first lie came from the mouths of you kids! Mackenzie, you were first, only because you were older and talking sooner. You weren't even three years old yet— pure, innocent, and a cute bundle of joy. You already had a treat after dinner and you wanted more, but Mom and I said no. About thirty minutes later I found you in your room with another cookie in your hand. As soon as you saw me, you swiftly swung your hand behind your back. I asked, "Did you take another cookie?" (It was a dumb question; I could see the cookie! I should have asked why you took another cookie.) You said, "No!" I was so surprised, I started to laugh. There you stood with the evidence in your hand and you said, "No!" I thought to myself, *Who taught you to do that? Must have been Mommy!* (Just kidding.)

The truth is, no one taught you to lie. It is part of our human nature. It's not part of what God places in our hearts, but something that we are born with. The good news is that with Jesus' help, we can choose not to lie by choosing to tell the truth. When you think it through, no one teaches a two-year-old to lie. No one! We are born with the ability and the temptation. I don't remember when I was two or three, but I'm sure I told a lie too.

John-Peter, not so fast, bucko. You aren't off the hook either. The first lie I can remember was when you were a little older, about four, I think. You have always loved to play games and to win. We were playing a simple card game, and I saw you looking in the deck to find when the card you wanted would come up. You were just two feet from me. I said, "John-Peter, did you look at those cards?" (I was still not asking very smart questions!) You said, "No!" I replied, "John, I saw you!" You quickly said with confidence, "It must have been someone else!" I laughed so hard! There wasn't anyone else in the room.

Kids, sometimes adults tell lies, and we shouldn't. We know better. It's a choice for us too. I can tell you that lying is always wrong, and it never makes the situation better, not to men-

tion the fact that God is disappointed. Telling the truth is so much better and always pleases God. This is what I want you to learn too.

Honesty with yourself is where you begin. Being honest with yourself about all of life's circumstances is important. It's easy at times to rationalize, to make yourself think something is okay, when you know it really isn't. I was at a grocery store with a friend, and he put thirty-five cents into the newspaper machine. He opened the door and took two newspapers. I asked him why he took two when he paid for only one. He said, "Aw, it's no big deal. This paper costs the newspaper company only a few pennies, and besides everyone does it." You see, he wasn't honest

The good news is that with Jesus' help,
we can choose not to lie by
choosing to tell the truth.

with himself. He knew better, but he rational-ized the situation so he could do what he wanted to do. Being dishonest with yourself in the little things leads to being dishonest with yourself in the big things. I don't want to over-dramatize, but I want you to remember that, eventually, you will get caught. The price for lying is high. You may "win" in a worldly way, but your heart will always hurt when you lie. You will always lose more than you gain.

Honesty with God is also important. This lying amuses me the most. People lie to God as if He doesn't know the real truth. God knows everything. It's the greatest privilege and blessing in the world to be able to always tell the truth to a grace-giving God who loves you just the way you are. You can confess your sins, tell Him how you really think and feel, and know that He will always love you. God expects honesty and will bless you for it.

Honesty with others is the outcome of being honest with yourself and honest with God. Someone once wisely said, "Honesty is

the best policy." I believe that, and the Bible says in Ephesians 4:15 that we are to speak the truth in love. It's not only important that we tell the truth, but that we do so in a loving way.

Honesty keeps your heart pure, your con-science clear, and you don't have to remember what you said. Honesty brings blessing into your life and into the lives of others. In my first job interview after college I was competing with several guys for one job opening as a private investigator. The owner of the company asked me many questions, but one stuck out in my mind. He asked if I would be willing to "bend the truth," if needed, to solve a big case. I said no. The owner said I was the youngest applicant and least experienced, but I got the job because of my commitment to honesty. He said he knew that if I was committed to telling the truth to others, he could count on my being honest with him too. I got my first job out of college largely due to my commitment to honesty.

Love,

Dad

Positive Attitude | Dr. Les Parrott III

Codirector of Center for Relationship Development, Seattle Pacific University; Seattle, Washington
Written to his first son, John Leslie

Dear John Leslie:

You were born one week ago tonight—February 8, 1998. And I've got to be honest, I'm not used to being a dad. I actually thought I had more time to prepare. But just seven nights ago you came into this world three months ahead of schedule—weighing just one and a half pounds. Your mom and I prayed for you long before you arrived, and now that you are here, we know that God has given us a very special son.

Just two days ago as your mom and I moved our belongings home from the hospital, we were looking at the dozens of cards, flowers, and gifts from friends around the country and noticed a baby gift from God right out our front door. It was a remarkable, pristine rainbow. It was a sign of promise that

God would be with us—and you—as you join our family. We named it John's Rainbow. And I doubt we'll ever look at another rainbow again without thinking of you.

As I write this letter, you are resting in an isolette at the neonatal unit in one of the finest hospitals on the West Coast. The tubes, monitors, lights, and alarms surrounding your bed don't faze you much, but the medical staff give them and you constant attention. Your entire body can fit in one of my hands, and my wedding band can easily slip over your entire arm and up to your shoulder. Your mother and I have spent many hours holding your head and feet, heeding the doctor's recommendation not to overstimulate you with too much rubbing and talking for now. We sing an occasional song and say short prayers. We'll have time for talking later.

Your grandfather, or Papa as he likes to be called, said a special prayer for you as he and I hovered over your tiny body this afternoon. You held on to one of my fingertips with surprising strength as he asked God to empower the nurses and doctors who are helping you grow. Papa, by the way, is the one who gave you your name.

John, you and I are just getting to know each other, but already, in a matter of days, I know I like you. You are a part of my family. You belong with me, the two of us together. We have a lot to learn about each other, but one thing I know about you for sure: you like

a challenge. The doctors tell us that only a very small percentage of babies your size enter the world the way you did. This very fact sets up a series of hurdles too numerous to mention, but in just seven days you're already working hard to overcome them.

Each day as I study you from head to toe, I pause to watch your little chest move in and out, each breath synchronized with a meter that measures your oxygen. And each day your breathing has improved. Three days ago they examined your brain to find it functioning just the way it should. Your small eyes have opened a time or two to let us know you are alert. Your mother and I know there will be

I hope and pray that you would incorporate a quality of character into your attitudes that enables you to adjust to things beyond your control.

setbacks—that's a part of improving and growing. But I have a very strong feeling you are up for the challenge.

I have confidence in you, John. And if there is one thing I hope and pray for you today—seven days after being born—it is that you would grow up to be physically healthy and strong, and that you would incorporate a quality of character into your attitudes that enables you to adjust to things beyond your control. This single ability will help you meet all of life's challenges more than any quality I know. It has to do with finding a positive attitude in spite of negative circumstances. You are learning far too early that life isn't always easy, that circumstances can justify a negative attitude if we let them. But I promise you that a negative attitude is a luxury you'll never be able to afford. The price is always defeat and failure.

Someday when you are old enough to appreciate and understand the story, I'll tell you how Papa learned the value of this attitude when he was a young man about my age. It's an inspiring story. And I promise that when circumstances in my life seem unfair, I will do my best to model for you the ability to adjust to things beyond my control. But as a brand-new father, John, I ask for patience and a little grace when I fail.

I love you so much, and I'm optimistic about your future. Before I close this letter I want to make a suggestion. When you are old enough, when you are beginning to see the value of a positive attitude in meeting life's challenges, I want you to visit a neonatology unit. I want you to see how far you've come. And if you are willing, I'd like to make that visit with you.

For right now, my dear son, I ask only that you rest. Tomorrow holds enough challenges for your tiny frame.

Your proud father,

Dad

One hundred years from now
it will not matter what kind of car I drove,
what kind of house I lived in,
how much money I had in my bank account,
or what my clothes looked like.
But one hundred years from now
the world may be a little better because
I was important in the life of a child.

Anonymous

What Will You Stand For? | Dan Reiland

Dear John-Peter,

One of my favorite movies is *Dead Poets Society*. Robin Williams portrays a passionate English professor, John Keating, who inspires his students to live life to the fullest, exclaiming, "Carpe diem, lads! Seize the day. Make your lives extraordinary!" Keating is a wonderful teacher. He cares about his students. His influence changes their lives forever, for the good. The challenge is that he is teaching in an Ivy League prep school that is stuck in tradition. Conformity is the rule. Thinking is not encouraged. Keating's style is not accepted.

In one of my favorite moments in the movie, Keating instructs the boys to rip some pages right out of a poetry textbook in the middle of class. After one student reads a few paragraphs about the mechanics of poetry, Keating tells the boys it's a bunch of bologna. "Rip it out!" he exclaims. The students are wide-eyed and look around at one another in disbelief, then they tear the pages out of the book. Do you know what he was teaching the boys, John-Peter? He was teaching them to think for themselves, which is one of the most valuable gifts anyone can receive.

What Keating didn't know (but wouldn't care anyway) was that one of the members of the faculty was looking in the window of his classroom when they did that. Those kinds of creative and effective learning experiences were not "acceptable" in the school. They were outside the box. Eventually Keating was in trouble and was forced to leave the school. The boys were heartbroken. They loved their teacher and appreciated all he taught them.

The most powerful scene in the movie is at the very end. Keating is in the classroom for the very last time, picking up his things and saying good-bye. The new teacher is already in the room. As Keating is going out the door, one of the boys stands up on his desk and exclaims, "O Captain! My Captain!" (That is a Walt Whitman poem about Abraham Lincoln.) He is standing up for what he believes. In this case for whom he believes. He is saying to his teacher, "I love you and believe in you and thank you for how you have changed my life." He is saying, "I am with you, and I believe in how you taught me to think for myself. I am willing to pay the consequences of not getting off my desk." One by one the other boys stand up on their desks. All the while the new teacher is yelling at the boys, ordering them to sit down, but they won't. They reveal the depth of their conviction. They remain standing for what they believe in.

My dear John-Peter, what will you stand for? As you get older, this will mean more to you, but I want to plant the seed now. Even now you are making decisions about what you will stand for. The list of things should not be long, but they must be deep in your heart.

You and I have talked much already about being an influencer, about being a leader. My desire for you is that you will not only stand, but be the first to stand. Be the leader wherever you go and whatever you do.

> My desire for you is that you will not only stand, but be the first to stand. Be the leader wherever you go and whatever you do.

Son, do not be a follower; do not follow the crowd. A crowd never knows where it's going.

You have noticed by now I have not told you *what* to stand for. You must choose for yourself. Be a free thinker and obey only God. You know that I believe in loving family, being a giver, and pouring your life into others, and I will continue to guide you with what I believe are godly and valuable life principles. Not so long from now, however, you must decide what is important to you and *stand up*. Don't look around to see if others are standing. Stand up for what is important to you. I will stand with you, and even for you if need be, until you are old enough and ready. The day may come when you stand for something different from what I do. We may not agree. I value your right to think and act creatively on your own far more than agreeing with me.

Keep your eyes on God, and stand up, my son, stand up.

I love you,

Dad

Choices | Dr. T. Garrott Benjamin Jr.

Bishop and Senior Pastor of Light of the World Church; Indianapolis, Indiana
Written to his sons, Thomas, Channing, and Christopher

The need for a father is as crucial as the need for a son, and the search of each for the other—through all the days of one's life—exempts no one. Happy is the man who finds both.

—Max Lerner

My dear sons,

As I write you, my heart is happy because I have been blessed with three wonderful sons. My heart is heavy because I know I didn't do enough, say enough, be enough to prepare you for the future. I hope one day I will stand tall enough in your memory to merit the words of Edgar Guest, who said, "I know he was as fine a dad as any boy ever had. What I didn't know until too late was the depth of his wisdom and the magnitude of his sacrifice."

First and foremost, Daddy loves his boys, and if you remember one thing from this letter, remember I love you more than you know and probably more than I show.

You were born to make the world a better place to live. Your true identity is a child of God, and yet each of you is special. Jesus said, "Without Me you can do nothing" (John 15:5). Howard Thurman, one of my mentors, said to me, "When you and God become one, all of life's resources begin to flow toward you." Discover your purpose and you discover your power.

I have found that if you *do what you love to do*, then you will do it well and everything else will follow. What you really want to do is *help people* (serve) and be happy. Jesus said, "Seek first the kingdom of God and His righteousness, and all these things shall be added to you" (Matt. 6:33).

The most important choice you will ever make is to choose Jesus Christ. God chose you, but you must choose God as your eternal Father and your King. You must submit to your King, Jesus, in everything. As I have told you, your quality of life depends on the *choices* you make. Your great-grandmother used to say, "If you make your bed of rocks, you will have to lie on them." I said in my book *Boys to Men*, which I dedicated to you, "There are no bad boys, just bad choices." I also said, "Success comes in cans: I can, I can, I can."

The second choice is your lifelong mate.

Your wife will be the mother of your children and your divinely designated helper in your family and every other area. My advice is similar to retired General Colin Powell's advice to the West Point cadets: "Marry high!" I agree, except I would be more specific: marry a woman who loves God *more* than she loves you. That's exactly what I did when I married your mother.

The third choice is your friends. Choose them carefully because the people you draw to you and around you are *the soil in which you grow*. Make sure your friends love and serve God, and if they don't, introduce them to Jesus. Be courageous enough to make new

As I have told you, your quality of life depends on the *choices* you make.

friends if the old ones don't cause you to grow and glow.

The fourth choice is your attitude. Chuck Swindoll says, "Attitude is everything." Carter G. Woodson, the father of African-American history, declared, "If you can control a man's thinking, then you can control his action." The proverbial writer observed, "As he thinks in his heart, so is he" (Prov. 23:7). That's why it is important to get all the education you can. You should read, travel, and explore. Expand your mind!

The fifth choice is giving. Giving is the secret to abundantly receiving. Motivator Zig Ziglar says, "Give enough people in this life what they need, and they will give you all you need." Jesus was even more succinct when He said, "The measure you give will be the measure you get" (Matt. 7:2 RSV). Adopt giving as a lifestyle. You are blessed to be a blessing.

I know it wasn't easy to be a PK (preacher's kid) but never discount the truth I preached to you and others. And never think

because you were raised in the church, you don't need the church. Soon I will be in heaven, and my prayer is that you don't forget to live your life and express your faith in such a way that we will spend eternity together.

You have given me so much joy and so much fulfillment as a dad. At the age of five, I was put on a train leaving St. Louis, Missouri, to live with my grandmother in Cleveland, Ohio, because my parents were getting a divorce. I felt rejected and unprotected. I promised the Lord I would do better with my sons. I have been the husband of one wife, your mother, for more than thirty years. We have loved each other through thick and thin with a lifelong commitment. Keeping your word is very important. It's called integrity.

Keep God first in your life. Love God with everything you have. Love your neighbor as you love yourself. Remember you are special, and you can make a difference in your lifetime. Keep a positive attitude. Give; it's the key to life. Serve; it's the key to peace. Pray; it's the key to power. Love; it's the key to God. Take care of your parents when they are unable to care for themselves.

Aim high in all you do, because Benjamin E. Mays, the educator, has said it well: "Low aim is sin!" You used to chuckle when I would say this, but it's still true:

> *Bite off more than you can chew and*
> *   chew it.*
> *Do more than you can do and do it.*
> *Hitch your wagon to a star.*
> *Take a seat and there you are!*

Daddy loves his boys. I really do, and all I ever wanted was the best for you. Aim high!
Love,
Dad

Forgiveness and Grace | Dan Reiland

Dear Mackenzie and John-Peter,

Your mom taught you to say to each other at an early age, "I'm sorry. Will you forgive me?" This lesson of forgiving and being forgiven is one of the most important you will ever learn. Ephesians 4:32 says that we are to forgive others as God in Christ has also forgiven us. Because God has forgiven you of your mistakes, you, too, must forgive others.

It's all about grace. Grace means receiving something we don't deserve. When you do something wrong, you don't deserve to be forgiven; you deserve to be punished. But grace says that even though you deserve to be punished, I will forgive you. We can give this grace, this forgiveness, to one another because God first forgave us through His Son, Jesus.

When I was a little boy, about five years old, I picked up my mom's ceramic piggy bank full of hundreds of pennies. She told me to put it down quickly because it was very heavy and I might drop it. It was fragile and handed down in the family for nearly one hundred years. I insisted I could handle it. I couldn't, and within a few seconds of lifting it about to my waist, I instantly realized it was too heavy for me. I dropped it, and it broke into a thousand pieces. I felt terrible. I deserved to be punished, but my mom forgave me. She even gave me all the pennies inside the bank. That's grace.

It's not always easy to forgive others. Sometimes you won't feel like it, but you must forgive anyway. You may even be hurt deeply one day, but you must forgive anyway. It's okay if you can't forgive completely—immediately. That's being honest about how you feel, but you must forgive, even if it takes you some time. I hope most of life's injustices will be small, and you will be large enough to forgive and forget quickly.

Forgiving someone is not about ignoring your feelings and pretending nothing happened. Sometimes you will need to tell God about the hurt, and sometimes you must lovingly confront the person who offended you. In all cases, however, it's with the aim of forgiving, not getting even, making him feel bad, or giving him a piece of your mind.

It's not always easy to forgive yourself. You may be harder on yourself than others. Remember that God forgives you and loves you, no matter what, and so do I. If we can forgive you, you can forgive yourself.

Forgiveness brings healing to the heart. Forgiving others brings healing to their hearts and to yours as well. Choosing not to forgive someone begins to eat away at your heart. Lack of forgiveness is like a cancer; it eats away at you from the inside. You can become unhappy and even bitter. There is no point to it. It is fruitless. Forgiveness brings healing and joy. Forgive and live!

In His Grace,

Dad

Because God has forgiven you of your mistakes, you, too, must forgive others.

Regrets and Relationships | Dr. Edwin Louis Cole

President, Christian Men's Network; Dallas, Texas
Written to his grandchildren, Sarah, Kendal, Lindsay, Bryce, Brandon, Joshua, and Seth

Dear kids,

My father never had the wonderful privilege of seeing his grandchildren, your moms and dads. He wanted so desperately to see them, but he died before any of them were born.

When life is over, at whatever age you may be, one thing you leave behind is regrets. I have had the privilege of not only watching your parents grow and mature, but also seeing you birthed and maturing into your teens and twenties. And if I continue to live, I will see my great-grandchildren as well.

I certainly will not leave behind any regrets about my relationship with you. Proverbs says that the glory of children is their father, but the glory of grandfathers is their grandchildren (17:6). That is so true.

Your grandmother and I love you, and we are so proud of you. You are a real joy to us. We have cherished each moment we have had with you. But there is one incredible truth you need to know, and I want to share it with you from my heart.

Because of Jesus, we have the glorious hope of continuing our relationship in heaven. It doesn't have to end. Being together again as a family is a wonderful thought. The truth that our relationship will last forever is marvelous.

So, one of these days when I'm gone, remember that I will be waiting for you to join me. Stay close to Jesus. Never leave His family of faith. Then and there, I'll be able to listen to every word about every detail of everything you want to tell me for as long as you want to talk.

My only regret would be finding in your lives some of the things I am not pleased with in my life. In hopes of preventing that from happening and enabling you to be free, I ask you to forgive me so you can release those things from your lives.

I love you too much to think that I might contribute anything to your lives that is not filled with God's grace and glory. My life has been lived serving God, preaching His gospel, and doing His will. This is the example I desire to be for you.

My life has been filled with adventure, surprises, friendships, and God's presence that has made everything worthwhile. Grandmother and I have had a precious marriage, and I grew to love her in a way I never thought possible.

We watched your moms and dads grow up and mature in body, mind, and spirit. We saw them follow the Lord and enter the ministry, and together we formed a great team. My hope and prayer are that you will find the same fulfillment in life.

Our only legacy to you is our greatest contribution. It is the greatest gift of all—faith in Christ. We give you that legacy, that you might follow Him as we learned to do, and have a life rich in eternal truths and blessings.

I love you and pray God's best for you,
Grandfather

Because of Jesus,
we have the glorious hope
of continuing our relationship in heaven.

Loving God and Loving Others | Dan Reiland

Dear Mackenzie and John-Peter,

Watching you kids grow up, who and what you love, and how you love has been a joy for me. You've moved so quickly from loving Big Bird and Barney to superstar sports icons such as Michael Jordan and Chipper Jones. Soon it will be boyfriends and girlfriends!

As you've matured, I've enjoyed watching how you've loved Grandfather and Grandmother Diaz (Pop and Mamu) with deep devotion, affection, and consistency. When we moved from San Diego to Atlanta, it was clear you missed them the most. I'm proud of you for that, but I believe it's because they first loved you. Mamu and Pop have loved you unconditionally and sacrificially since the day you were born. They play with you by the hour and give you wonderful gifts. They encourage you and believe in you. They listen to you. They care for you and love you with all their hearts.

This is how God loves you, with all His heart and devotion. He loved you so much He gave His only Son to die on a cross so that you could live with Him forever in heaven. There is no greater love! Jesus said, "'You shall love the LORD your God with all your heart, with all your soul, and with all your mind.' This is the first and great commandment. And the second is like it: 'You shall love your neighbor as yourself'" (Matt. 22:37–39). God loved you first, and He loves you just the way you are.

God wants you to love Him more than anyone or anything else. I want you to love Him that way too.

Learning to love God is connected to obeying God and often moves through three stages. The first is out of fear. You obey God for fear of the consequences of what may happen if you don't. This is an immature love and lacks understanding of God's grace. It's similar

God wants you to love Him more than anyone or anything else. I want you to love Him that way too.

to behaving well in school because you may be sent to the principal's office and be punished if you don't. The second stage is connected to duty or responsibility. You obey God because you know it's right. You do the right thing out of discipline and character. This is similar to doing your homework not because you want to, but because you know it's the right thing to do. The final stage is motivated by love itself. You love God so much that you obey Him just because you want to please and honor Him. This is similar to bringing your mom flowers just to warm her heart or cleaning your room just to make her smile.

Loving God with all your heart, soul, and mind means putting Him first. Loving God means you don't love anything more than Him. Sometimes this is hard. We are very human and get sidetracked easily. Don't be discouraged or give up; just keep loving Him. Remember, He loved you first, and He will never stop loving you. Two things will help you love God more and more. First is prayer and second is reading the Bible. Both help you know who God is, and that helps you love Him more.

When you begin to understand how much God loves you, you can begin to love yourself the way God intended. God wants you to love yourself—not so much that you are conceited, and not so little that you are discouraged, but just the way He loves you. In other words, love and appreciate yourself because God does and He created you in a "wonderful" way. You can't give to others what you don't possess inside yourself. You can't love others if you don't love yourself.

Loving others is sometimes difficult. As brother and sister, you love each other, but every once in a while you argue and get upset with each other. That's normal as long as it doesn't last long, you are able to forgive, and you make up. You can even get mad at God! That's okay! But don't stay upset too long. It's better to make up and continue to love.

Loving others requires putting them first. Love is a joy and privilege, but it does require sacrifice. When your mom and I were first married in 1981, we moved from California to Kentucky. We were moving to Wilmore, a little town near Lexington, to finish my last year of seminary. Wilmore had one gas station, one bank, one grocery store, one dry cleaner, and one raggedy-looking town dog. Your mom doesn't like small towns and didn't

want to live there. I loved Wilmore and needed to finish seminary. She moved with me because she loved me and was willing to put me first. She still had some classes left to graduate from college, and she put them on hold until we returned to San Diego. As soon as we were back, she went back to college and finished her degree.

Loving others takes effort. You have to think about it. We all need to be intentional about loving others. Think about celebrating birthdays. We celebrate someone's birthday because we love him or her. The party is fun, but it takes some effort and planning to make it special.

God has taught me more about loving others through having and loving you than anything or anyone else. Loving you is one of the greatest joys of my life.

I love you,

Dad

Above all cares of this life,
let our ardent anxiety be to mould the
minds and manners of our children.

John Quincy Adams

Do the Right Thing | Pastor Abel Ledezma

Director of Hispanic Ministry, INJOY Stewardship Services; San Diego, California
Written to his two children, Abel and Damaris

Dear Abel and Damaris,

As I reflect back to the days when both of you were born, I have to say that those two moments have been the greatest moments of my life. I never imagined how my life would change just by becoming your dad. I have watched you both grow into full-grown Christians serving God with all your hearts. The journey has made proud parents of your mom and me. However, there will still be more lessons to learn in life as you continue to grow and face the future with courage.

Once I heard my friend John Maxwell teach on the principle of facing life's challenges, and now I would like to pass this wisdom on to you as you face life's challenges. John stated, "It is not what happens to me that matters, but what happens in me." The

message to glean from those few words is simplistic in nature but profound in impact. You will not be able to control what other people will do or how they will behave or what will happen around you. But you do control what will happen in you and how you will react. That choice is up to you.

My constant prayer is that you will keep your hearts pure, well guarded from all the things that can hurt and hinder you from growing and learning. Doing the right things in life is a challenge in itself, but the rewards are great. You must maintain a focus on your life's goal, but the journey you will experience on the way to the goal will have a greater impact on your life than the goal itself. Your relationship with God, yourself, and others will determine the characteristics and quality of your journey. You must know who you are and what your strengths and weaknesses are. Assess and evaluate within yourself the areas that need to be changed or strengthened.

Here are some of the key areas to think through and questions to ask yourself. God: Is my relationship with Him as it should be? Life: What is my personal perspective? What am I investing in it? What do I need to "give up" in order to "go up"? Other people: Am I treating them as I want to be treated? Am I burning my bridges behind me, or am I keeping the roads open? Am I building people up or taking for granted the friends I have around me?

I want to remind both of you about some common values to live by. First, always have a strong commitment to God. Remember that He is the source for your life. He gives you strength to continue and hope for your future. Being committed to God above all else will keep you in balance. Second, make a personal commitment to live a God-honoring life. Make it your goal to strive for God's standard, not worldly standards. Third, maintain a strong commitment to yourself and family. Personal and family values will keep you focused on worthy things. Fourth, challenge yourselves to go the extra mile. Don't go with the pace; bet-

Remember that the good you do today may be forgotten tomorrow, but do good anyway!

ter yet, become a pacesetter. Your example will take other people to a higher level.

Attitude can make a big difference in every situation. The proper attitude will help you do the right things. Don't ever do something simply because it *feels* as though it is the right thing to do. Do it because it is the right thing to do. There is a difference. Often the right thing is not the easiest thing to do. If you keep the right attitude about God, yourself, family, friends, work, and life, your choices will be sound, and the proper actions will follow. Last, remember that the good you do today may be forgotten tomorrow, but do good anyway! And know that you honor God when you do the right thing.

With love,
Your dad

The Value of Integrity | Dan Reiland

Dear Mackenzie and John-Peter,

A local TV news station conducted an interesting experiment. The news team hid eleven wallets around Atlanta and filmed the people who found them. What do you think the people did? Kept them or turned them in? Well, there were some of each. It was surprising, in particular, to see who kept the wallets. Each situation had the same setup—a wallet with money that didn't belong to the finder. The outside circumstances were the same, but what was on the inside of each person's character was different. What's inside makes all the difference.

Integrity is a part of your character that determines whether you will do right or wrong when you know what is right. Integrity guides you to do what is right even when no one is looking. The people who found the wallets and kept them thought no one was looking. They did not have integrity. The people who found the wallets and returned them to their rightful owners had integrity. Integrity helps you make the right choices in life.

I was teaching a lesson on the apostle Paul's leadership from Acts 27 to the Skyline Church staff. It was a brilliant lesson and the staff loved it. It was brilliant because Chuck Swindoll wrote it. I had his tape series and so enjoyed the lesson that I taught it to the staff. As I finished the lesson, the staff generously lavished praise on me. I was tempted to be silent, to let them think I wrote it. But a little voice inside my heart said, "Give credit to the original author." I wrestled with the issue for nearly a minute (I'm not proud that I had to think about it), but I did the right thing. I gave credit to Chuck Swindoll, as he deserved. After the meeting, Pastor Maxwell pulled me aside, put his arm on my shoulder, and said, "I was wondering what you would do." I asked, "What do you mean?" He replied, "I have that tape too!"

Doing the right thing should be motivated not by the possibility of being caught, but by a heart to please God and be true to yourself. A young man named Jeremy was recently sent to prison for experimenting with drugs while in the army. Jeremy is a good Christian man, happily married, and had a flawless record in the army and in civilian life. He was raised in a wonderful home and is respected in his church. He made a foolish but brief mistake experimenting with drugs with some other men in the army. The army has a zero tolerance rule on drugs. So, despite the numerous testimonies of many who believe in and support Jeremy, the army gave him seven months in prison and a bad-conduct discharge. It was a harsh punishment, in my opinion, for a young man who served above and beyond the call of duty and earned medals for that service. Jeremy had a choice when his superior officer asked him if he used drugs. He could have said no and escaped all consequences, as his fellow soldiers did. The others lied; they did not demonstrate integrity. Jeremy knew that living with a heavy heart

Doing the right thing should be motivated by a heart to please God and be true to yourself.

and not pleasing God were more significant than receiving punishment from the army. He knew that the right thing to do was tell the truth, no matter what. I'm proud of Jeremy, and I respect him because he made the right choice, a tough choice, one of integrity. He had the integrity to face his mistake with courage and honor. He is a man of integrity.

One of the Joshua's Men asked me on a retreat if integrity could be developed and if so, how. What a great question—a tricky question! Either way could lead you to believe that some people have more integrity than others. I believe this is faulty thinking and even dangerous thinking because you could excuse certain wrong behavior because your integrity wasn't yet developed enough. It's faulty thinking because character is not a number or an amount; it's a condition of the heart. It's not like a certain skill level in your golf game. It's more like hitting the little ball into the hole. Either you did or you didn't.

Consistency of integrity is important.

Some folks have integrity in some areas of their lives but not in others. This leads to trouble. They will cheat on some holes, but not on others. This is not about perfection, so the picture is not one of a life of "holes in one." Life is more like an ongoing series of strokes. In each one you do your best to hit the ball straight toward the target. Back to my friend's question about developing integrity. I told him I didn't know the answer, but I do know that integrity can be practiced as a lifestyle. You can have a heart of integrity by making a commitment to honesty and obedience to God and by doing your very best. Kids, just keep hitting the ball as straight as you can.

Love,

Dad

Lessons in Life from the Art of Fishing | Dr. Tony Zeiss

President, Central Piedmont Community College; Charlotte, North Carolina
Written to his sons, Brett and Bryan

Dear Brett and Bryan,

As the two of you enter adulthood, your mother and I have been thinking about some important things in life we want to be sure you know.

Each of us needs to determine what is significant and to decide how we will live. This sounds simple, but can be ever so complex at times. Perhaps a template for the process of living will be useful to you. I hope you'll enjoy a mental fishing trip with your old dad since you both grew up with fishing rods in your hands.

A basic thing about fishing (or living) is to establish a vision for what you want to accomplish and then plan your approach. Do you want to become the best fisherman in your area of fishing interests? What will

you go fishing for: bass, trout, stripers, or marlin? Your technical approach will change depending upon your objective. Your fundamental approach, however, should remain consistent, regardless of the quarry. For instance, you know that you must be alert and optimistic even when the fish aren't biting. How many times have you missed a strike because you took a mental hike or slipped into negative thinking? Staying alert and being optimistic are essential elements of a successful fishing trip. A favorite proverb advises that he who has a merry heart has a continual feast. Once you have established your vision and determined your mental approach, stick with them. On the vision thing, think *big!* There is power in vision, so don't shortchange yourself.

To catch fish, you have to take the time to learn how to fish well. You have to put in hours of practice and observe the techniques of others. When you make mistakes, such as casting badly, leaving the plug out of the boat, or forgetting the sunscreen, it is healthy to admit them and important to learn from them. You also realize that becoming a really skilled fisherman involves a lifetime of learning. There is no finish line to self-improvement.

All fishermen experience times when things just don't go as planned. The boat's motor won't start; you get backlashes galore; a cloudburst makes the water so muddy it's too thick to drink and too thin to plow. In times like these, look for the cloud's silver lining. Put the whole thing in perspective: How important will that temperamental motor, the backlashes, or the rain be a hundred years from now? How about ten years or ten months or even ten days from now? Besides, all fishing trips, even ones that are fraught with adversity, add to your experience and ultimately help you become a better fisherman. Another way to look at adversity is to ask yourself if it threatens your soul, your life, or your family. If not, then you probably have little to worry about. Indeed, our Lord, the greatest fisherman of all time, told us to cast our anxiety on Him.

On the vision thing, think *big!* There is power in vision, so don't shortchange yourself.

When you hook a nice fish, play it for the pure enjoyment of the moment. Fishing is meant to be enjoyed, relished, and remembered during times when this wonderful pastime seems far away. Stay focused and keep a tight line, even when you are tired. Persistence boats more fish than all the luck or wishes in the world.

On some days it seems nothing can go wrong. The fish are feeding on everything you toss at them. Remember the white bass on Stillhouse Hollow or black bass fishing with Grandpa and Randy, Brett? How about all those bass and the huge walleye on Pueblo Reservoir, Bryan? Of course, we can't forget that marlin off Cabo San Lucas or those beauties off Big Pine Key. Such times are great, but I have observed that success often breeds arrogance or complacency, sometimes both. I suppose each bright sky has a cloudy lining somewhere close by. Accept success with humility.

I hope you will remember to be kind to the small fish. Handle them gently, and return them to the comfort of their surroundings. Photograph your prize fish when you can, and leave them to catch another day. Respect them for their wisdom and perseverance; they didn't become large by being stupid or lazy. Be thankful for all fish and for all opportunities to fish. This fishing business, like living and salvation, is a privilege, a gift from the Almighty.

Don't forget to do some reflecting while you are out on your favorite trout stream or on your special lake. Consider your blessings, your family, your relationships, and what kind of person you are becoming—the meaningful things of life.

While you're at it, remember the legacies of the grandfathers and grandmothers who fished before you. They helped you learn the fine art of fishing; they left you a gift greater than gold and finer than silver—your good name.

Finally, I know you will be great fishermen all of your lives, ever improving. But remember that catching bigger and bigger fish is not the real measure of a life. The real measure is learning to translate your successes into significance for others: to be able to pass along, especially to your children, what you have learned about the finer points of tying flies, selecting lures, and retrieving with finesse. Remember that all things happen for good to those who love our Lord, that He will be with you and yours always, and that no lake or stream will ever be remote enough to separate you from the love your mother and I have for you. Thanks for being such great fishermen!

Love,
Dad

Never Give Up | Dan Reiland

Dear Mackenzie and John-Peter,

During a Saturday afternoon game, a young boy about six years old was up to bat in his first T-ball game. He swung three times with all his might but just couldn't hit the ball. No matter how hard he tried, the ball just sat there on top of the plastic tee, daring him to hit it. Finally, in exasperation, he looked back at his dad, then out at his coach, then he did the most amazing thing. He swatted the ball off the tee with his hand and ran to first base while everyone cheered him on!

There is much to learn about determination and perseverance from that little boy. We can learn the value of never giving up.

The first thing we can learn about not giving up is that you must have hope. As long as the ball still sat on the tee, there was a chance to hit it. Never give up; always take another swing.

A pastoral colleague and friend of mine, Dwayne Potteiger, discovered he had brain cancer. The news shocked all of us and devastated him, his wife, and their two precious lit-

Put your mind to it,
and you can accomplish
anything you want—if you never give up.

tle girls. Dwayne was so courageous. He endured radiation treatment, a "halo" screwed into his head, and three brain surgeries. Today, six years later, Dwayne is doing well. I'll never forget his words: "As long as I have hope, I can keep going one day at a time." It's true. Whether it's swinging a bat or battling brain cancer, hope is the key that keeps you going.

The second thing to learn is that giving up never solves anything. Quitting doesn't make the situation better and often makes things worse. If that little boy had walked out of the batter's box in frustration, nothing would have been solved. And it would have been more difficult for him to step up to the plate next time.

John-Peter, I remember a long time ago when you were learning to tie your shoes. You were so frustrated and wanted to give up. You said, "I can't." And I told you many times, "You can!" (I also said that "I can't" isn't allowed in the Reiland family—I know you remember that.) Can you imagine if you really gave up? You'd be seventeen years old asking your girlfriend to tie your shoes.

Another important thing to learn is that accomplishing the goal or task instead of giving up increases self-confidence and builds character. The next time up to bat, the lad swung the bat and smacked a good base hit. It's more than just hitting a ball; it's believing you can. It's the confidence and character within you to get back up to the plate in front of all those people to try again.

One more thing to learn is that there is a big difference between failing and giving up. I have a couple of friends who are great lawyers today; they didn't pass the bar exam the first time, but they didn't give up. A pastor friend of mine, Gerald Brooks, tells how he single-handedly "made a mess" of his first little church. Today Gerald is a very successful pastor of a church with more than two thousand in attendance in Plano, Texas. He failed forward by not giving up.

You will make mistakes and even fail at times in your life. That's okay. As a matter of fact, failing is good if you learn from your mistakes. If you aren't making mistakes and failing on occasion, you aren't taking enough risks and stretching toward your fullest potential. I failed my first driving test, which is probably no surprise to you. I drove the wrong way down a one-way street and managed to scare a wide-eyed older woman in a Ford Falcon half to death! I had just turned seventeen and had planned a special trip to Washington, D.C. I could still go, but could not drive myself. I was so disappointed, but I learned from the mistakes I made and I took it again. The second

time I scored 97 percent, which is the best score I will ever get for driving anything.

Abraham Lincoln is a vivid example of someone who never gave up. He was born in 1809. In 1816 his family was forced out of the home; he had to work to help support all of them. In 1818 (when Abe was only nine) his mother died. In 1831 he failed in business. In 1832 he ran for state legislature and lost. In 1832 he also lost his job; he wanted to go to law school but couldn't get in. In 1833 he borrowed some money from a friend to begin a business, and by the end of the year he was bankrupt. He took the next seventeen years to pay off his debt. In 1834 he ran for state legislature and won. In 1835 he was engaged to be married, his fiancée died, and his heart was broken. In 1836 he had a nervous breakdown and was in bed for six months. In 1838 he tried to become the speaker of the state legislature and was defeated. In 1840 he attempted to become elector and lost. In 1843 he ran for Congress and lost. In 1846 he ran for Congress again. He won and went to Washington and did a good job. In 1848 he ran for reelection to Congress but lost. In 1849 he sought the job of land officer in his home state and was rejected. In 1854 he ran for Senate of the United States and lost. In 1856 he sought the vice presidential nomination at his party's national convention and got less than one hundred votes. In 1858 he ran for U.S. Senate again, and again he lost. In 1860 he was elected president of the United States. Abraham Lincoln never gave up and he became president. Put your mind to it, and you can accomplish anything you want—if you never give up.

Love,

Dad

Fathers, do not provoke your children to wrath,
but bring them up in the training
and admonition of the Lord.

Ephesians 6:4

Legacy of Love | Rev. H. B. London Jr.

Vice President, Ministry Outreach / Pastoral Ministries, Focus on the Family; Colorado Springs, Colorado
Written to his four grandchildren, Taylor, Hilary, Amanda, and Jeffrey

Dear kids,

Life goes by so quickly, and the distance between us makes it nearly impossible for us to see you as much as Nana and I would like. Often when we're together, there is so much going on in the house that I never get around to telling you all the things that I feel in my heart.

I remember when you came to Colorado Springs to attend your great-grandfather London's funeral service. It was a sad time for all of us, but I was so proud of you. You were handsome and beautiful. You were well behaved, and people made a fuss over you. I thought then of the legacy you would be called to carry on even beyond your own moms and dads. You represent six generations of Londons who have served the church and carried high and courageously the banner of

Jesus Christ. You have been genuinely blessed.

You never knew Two-Papa. He was my grandfather, your great-great-grandfather. He really had more influence on me and my moral and spiritual development than any other person. I was his only grandson. He spoiled me and prayed for me. He told me fun stories and stood by me, no matter what.

One day he became ill, and I flew to visit him in Houston, Texas. I didn't know it, but it would be the last time I would ever see "my" papa. In fact, I told him that day how much I loved him and how grateful I had been for his love. I sat on his bed, put cold washcloths on his head, and gave him little sips of water. For that whole day we just loved each other. Our time together ended much too soon, and I had to go on to another city.

I remember the last conversation I ever had with your great-great-grandfather, and it was one that I will treasure all my life, one that I want to pass on to you.

You see, your papa (that's me) was at that time a very young and inexperienced pastor. I was just getting started in my ministry, and "my" papa was near the end of his. As I sat on the hospital bed and held his hand in mine, I asked him to tell me the secret of his most successful career. Why had he been so loved by so many? How had he gained so much acceptance? I wasn't sure if he could answer me or not. Because, you see, he had a really difficult time talking, but he did answer. He called

your papa "Junior" (I bet you never knew I used to be called Junior), and then he told me the secret of his long and anointed service. He said, "Junior, I learned a long time ago that it is one thing to tell people how much God loves them, but it's also very important for them to know how much you love them."

I know that may not sound like such a big deal, but, kids, that's how your great-great-grandfather taught me how to live my life, and I desperately want you to learn that lesson from me. Love God with all your heart. Talk to Him, listen to Him, obey Him, and cherish your relationship with Him, but whatever you do, let other people, especially your family,

Whatever you do, let other people, especially your family, know how much you love them.

know how much you love them. Treat every person you meet with respect, and remember that God loves him as though he were the only one in all the world to love—just as He does you. I only wish you had known "my" papa. That's the legacy he left me.

Oh, about that legacy that I want to pass on to you? It's a big word that means something received from an ancestor, but probably I can explain it to you in a better way. Just imagine I had something very valuable—let's say a gold watch or a ring or maybe even some pictures of your mom and dad that I want you to have one day. I would say to you—Taylor, Hilary, Amanda, Jeffrey—when the right time comes, these things that I value so much will be yours. I want you to keep them safe. Take good care of them because someday you will give them to your children. That's a legacy. It's something very valuable that you pass on from one family member to another.

For many, many years the London family has passed from one generation to the next a legacy more important than a gold watch or memorable pictures. It has been a legacy of love for one another. When Papa and Nana have gone to be with Jesus, your moms and dads will have a great responsibility to one another to continue that legacy of love. I learned a long time ago that if you know someone loves you, and you know you matter a lot to that someone else, you can make it through anything. We need to make sure we say to one another often, "I love you," and really mean it! Don't you agree?

Well, I had better keep moving, but I just wanted you to know how special you are to me. I'll love you forever, just as I love your folks, and I pray that you will always love one another too. You see, that's the legacy you will pass on. Now guess who really loves you? Right! Papa! And, of course, Jesus too! I wish you were here right now so I could give you a great big hug, but I'll see you soon.

Love,

Papa

Money Matters | Dan Reiland

Dear Mackenzie and John-Peter,

As your dad, I want to share with you some thoughts about money. First, I must tell you that I am not a financial wizard. I do have, however, a strong grasp on the basics that will provide for you a good foundation to understand, appreciate, and manage your money.

Money has an impact on people starting at a very early age. If it comes to you too easily, it may not mean much and you may not learn to appreciate it. If money comes to you by way of a great deal of difficulty, it may form too strong a grip on you for fear of losing it.

Money is a tool, not the goal. If you know what you want in life, money can help you get there. But never make money by itself your objective. If money is your goal, you will never have enough, and soon you will no longer own it because it will own you. When I was a teenager, I wanted an electric guitar more than

anything. I loved music and I wanted to be in a rock and roll band. I mowed lawns for more than a year and finally bought a Gibson SG deluxe electric guitar. I was on my way! We were living at Cardiff By the Sea, California, then, and some guys in a garage band called the Night Crew asked me to join the group. We actually played for our junior high school's big dance. (Those were back in the days when volume made up for talent.) I learned that money could help me achieve a dream.

Money cannot buy the best things in life, such as love, hope, friends, eternal life, happiness, and peace of mind. Now don't get me wrong, money is not evil or bad, and more is generally better than less—but only if you view it the right way. As I said, money is merely a tool. Money by itself means nothing. Used wisely, money can open many doors of positive and productive opportunities.

No doubt you will learn a much more sophisticated financial plan from financial experts, but I want to offer you the most basic plan that will serve you well. It's called the 10-10-80 plan. Give 10 percent to God, 10 percent to savings, and live on 80 percent. It works! You are better off giving more than 20 percent to God and savings, but this simple plan is a winner. This plan will never make you a wealthy individual, but violate it and you will have financial problems. If your basic living expenses are greater than 80 percent of your income, you are living above your means, and you are headed for serious financial trouble. Trust me. Nothing you can buy is worth

the tension and heartache that come from living with financial problems.

Invest in education over entertainment. Your mom and I have given up many concerts and ball games to travel to foreign countries such as South Africa and Israel and would do it again in a heartbeat. There is no comparison! Going out to dinner is great, but it doesn't hold a candle to the richness of learning and growing from foreign travel. Our lives are changed forever from our travel to the Holy Land. Walking where Jesus walked is better than having the finest entertainment money can buy. Education doesn't have to be so grand in nature. It may be books, tapes, seminars,

Used wisely, money can open many doors of positive and productive opportunities.

and postgraduate college classes. The point is, put your money in education—keep on learning and growing.

Invest in people over things. Your mom and I have given up many toys to help other people, and we don't regret it for a moment. Others have invested in us as well. Your grammy sent me to college and seminary. I'll never forget coming home in the early eighties from a gathering of young men called the Cadre, which Keith Drury had organized. We were a group of young leaders in whom Keith saw potential and committed to invest part of his life. We spoke briefly of a conference Keith wanted me to attend, and I desperately wanted to go but I didn't have two nickels to rub together at that time. The subject was dropped. On the way to the airport, Keith handed me a book and said, "Toss this in your briefcase and read it on the plane." I opened the book on the plane and found two one-hundred-dollar bills stapled to the cover with a note that said, "See you at the conference; I

believe in you." That had a deep impact on me, far beyond the conference. I knew Keith didn't have much money either, but he chose to invest in me.

Invest in what is eternal over what is temporary. Your mom and I have given up new cars to help build churches, and we sleep well at night knowing we've chosen the right thing. Long after the cars would be rusted piles of metal in some junkyard, our investment will literally live forever.

John Wesley said, "Make all you can, save all you can, give all you can." Make much and save much, but the best is giving. I believe you can't outgive God. Generosity is essential. Be generous, kids. Hold loosely to the things of this world. Be wise with your money, but remember that you came into this world with nothing and everything you have was given to you.

Love,
Dad

Starting Again | Dr. J. Allan Petersen

Founder of Family Concern, Inc.; Wheat Ridge, Colorado
Written to his grandson, Matthew

My dear Matt,

You have been on my heart lately, and I have felt an urging to write to you. I am concerned about some of your recent struggles. Finding our way in God's will is not an easy task, and yet I can only encourage you to continue your journey. The eventual, successful discovery of your vocation will more than make up for all the challenges of getting there. You may think no one understands the hurdles that are before you, but be assured, as a young man I, too, was faced with what seemed to be an endless uphill battle.

Principles of recovery. Of course, there is no one simple answer to the difficulties of life. There is no easy formula. Having faith in God and trusting Him with your future are important, but difficult questions still linger, such as, Where do I start? What do I let go of? What

do I hang on to? My desire in writing to you is to attempt to help you answer these questions.

First and most important, *you can begin again.* If Jesus taught us anything, it was that. You can rebuild something wonderful from your ashes. But it does begin with you. Wishes mean nothing without action. What you do proves what you really want and intend. You can be back on track again, but you must take responsibility for your problems and take action to change the situation.

Seek forgiveness, from yourself and anyone else involved. Forgiveness precedes restoration. Every thoughtful human being knows that wrongs must be righted if relationships are to survive. But because we are human, we sometimes fail. And since our failures often affect and hurt others, we all need forgiveness.

Consider the past and the future. The harvest we reap in the future will reflect what we sowed in the past. Effectiveness of today is determined by the healing and forgetting of yesterday. We all have a spotted history, checkered with failure, fracture, and foolishness. We can resign ourselves to its debilitating effects, or we can learn from it and build on it. Charles Kettering said, "You can fail forward."

It comes down to how you choose to position your past. Will your decision be to let it paralyze you or prompt you to do something better? Thomas Edison suffered what seemed an irreparable loss. His whole factory, with all his supplies, records, compounds, and equipment, was burning in an uncontrollable fire. Literally everything was being destroyed. With the fire barely under control, he called his employees together and made an incredible announcement. "We will rebuild." Later, he explained, "We can always make capital out of a disaster. We just clear out a bunch of old rubbish. We'll build bigger and better on the ruins." I know you well, and I believe you, too, will build on the ruins.

Speak your faith. This principle is revolutionary, Matt. Though it is woven into the very fabric and nature of man, it goes largely unrecognized. Few understand its powerful secret, and fewer still practice it in everyday life. The secret is words—right words, faith-filled words, spoken words—that open the door for

Finding our way in God's will is not an easy task, and yet I can only encourage you to continue your journey.

God to work, for miracles to happen. They become the link between desire and reality.

If you want to change something, you must believe it enough to speak it. Before you discredit this as some psychological ritual or cute little gimmick, you must understand why words work and why they are so powerful.

Recent findings in the field of neurology indicate that the speech center in the brain rules over all the other nerves. A person's speech nerve center has power over all of the body to manipulate it in the way he wishes. A neurosurgeon explains it this way: "If someone keeps on saying, 'I'm going to become weak,' then right away, all the nerves receive that message and say, 'Let's prepare to become weak, for we've received instructions from our control communication that we should become weak.' And they adjust their physical attitudes to weakness. If someone says, 'I have no ability; I can't do this job,' then right away all the nerves begin to declare the same thing and prepare themselves to be a part of an incapable person."

My friend Dr. Paul Yonggi Cho of Seoul, Korea, says, "What you speak you are going to get. If you keep on saying that you are poor, then all of your system conditions itself to attract poverty, and you will be at home in poverty; you would rather be poor. Before you can be changed, you must change your language. If you do not change your language, you cannot change yourself." The tongue is the least member of the body, James says, but it can bridle the whole body—for good or for ill.

Have a positive purpose. Focus on what you want to happen, not on what you don't want to happen. Your energies must be directed toward the positive, the productive, the excellent. Years ago I watched Karl Wallenda perform his death-defying stunts in the circus. Known as the Flying Wallendas, he, his wife, and his family were world famous. "Walking the tightrope is living—everything else is waiting" was his motto. In all his stunning career, he never feared falling. But on a high wire stretched between two downtown buildings in

San Juan, Puerto Rico, as thousands stared in disbelief, Karl fell to his death. His wife gave this explanation: "All Karl thought about for three straight months prior to it was falling. It was the first time he'd ever thought about that, and it seemed to me he put all his energies into not falling rather than walking the tightrope." You are drawn to the things you worry about. Worry is negative goal setting. When Wallenda poured his energies into not falling, instead of walking the tightrope, he was destined to fall.

Look to the future as full of potential. Your past is not your whole life. One dark chapter does not ruin the whole biography. You still have a full, bright future beyond your wildest dreams. Put your past where it belongs now—behind you—and press on for a positive future. I love you and believe in you.

Love,
Your grandfather

The words that a father speaks
to his children in the privacy of home
are not heard by the world,
but, as in whispering-galleries, they are clearly
heard at the end and by posterity.

Jean Paul Richter

Attitude Is Everything | Dan Reiland

Dear Mackenzie,

Millions of Americans watched an Olympic ice-skater complain and make a scene shortly after beginning her routine on the ice. She skated over to the judges to plead her case by whining about her shoes being untied or something! She skated again, no better, and took home no medal. In contrast, during the summer Olympics a courageous young gymnast competed with an injured ankle without so much as a whimper. Her vault was incredible, and she took home the gold!

Both were great athletes. The difference was in their attitudes. A bad attitude never makes the situation better. Having a bad attitude makes enjoying life on a daily basis nearly impossible.

Attitude is a choice. You choose how you will respond to the tough situations that life throws your way. A good friend of mine, named Todd Gross, has a fantastic attitude. He sometimes wears a pin on his shirt that simply says "attitude." At lunch one day, I asked him about the pin, and he said that it reminds him every day that a good attitude is a choice. I have seen Todd go through some tough situations, but always with a good attitude. His good attitude doesn't guarantee that everything will always work out perfectly, but it helps him make the best of even the tough times. The positive perspective a good attitude brings often turns a difficult situation into a blessing.

A good attitude is your responsibility. No one can have a good attitude for you. You can't buy one, and no one can give you one as a gift. A good attitude is a gift already placed within your mind and heart by God, just waiting for you to choose it on a daily basis. When you were a little girl, maybe five years old, I would tell you it was time for happy lips. That was my way of encouraging a smile from you. You began to learn at an early age that you could respond in a positive or negative way. No one else could do it for you.

Life isn't always easy, but a positive attitude is available in all circumstances. Some days are tough, but a positive attitude is always available, no matter how difficult the situation. I'd like to offer you some principles that help my attitude and will help yours too.

To change your attitude, you must change your thinking. If you don't like a subject in school and are not doing well in it, you must change how you think about the subject. Your attitude will get better, and you will do better in the class. Let's say you don't like math. You don't think it will help you in daily

Attitude is the key to success in life, and more significant, it is the key to happiness and true joy.

life, so your attitude sours on the subject. To change your thinking means to look at math differently, more as a game, challenge, or contest. Doing that will help you do better in the class, and you will be ahead in life.

To change your attitude, you need to associate with positive people. John Maxwell has taught me, and modeled for me more than anyone I know, how to have a good attitude. John not only makes lemonade out of lemons, but also makes enough to share with everyone around him! Find positive people with good attitudes, and make friends with them. Run from negative people. Run fast!

To change your attitude, you need to look for the positive. If you look hard enough, you can find the positive in every situation. Someone said, "Even a broken clock is right twice a day!" Keep looking!

To change your attitude, you need to develop a grateful heart. Ungrateful people do not have good attitudes. They are too focused on everything in life they don't have. Focus on

all the good things and blessings from God that you do have, and your attitude will blossom beautifully.

Attitude is the key to success in life, and more significant, it is the key to happiness and true joy. My sweet Mackenzie, I love you more than words can express, and I desire for you happiness and joy throughout your life. If I could buy it for you, I would sell everything I own (except maybe my Beatles albums) and give a good attitude to you today. But it is something you must find on your own. I commit myself and my love to be your number one encourager and champion for a good attitude. I know it's in you. I see it in you. Your heart is so precious. Just let it out. I promise you it's worth it. Remember, everyone is allowed a few of those rare but terrible, no-good, very bad, awful days, and even on those days, I love you big as the sky!

Always,
Your dad

Tremendous Life Principles | Charles E. "Tremendous" Jones

President of Executive Books / Life Management Services; Mechanicsburg, Pennsylvania
Written to his grandson, Sammy

My dear Sammy, Each word in this letter is bathed with my love and prayers for you. As you get older, you'll discover that your mind doesn't always keep pace with your body. The food you eat nourishes your body, but what you feed your mind and heart determines your growth as a person.

I'm going to share a few principles that I pray you'll commit to memory. I could share many more, but I've tried to select ones that I wish I could have begun working on earlier in my life.

Read, read, read, read, read. A proper diet is good for your body, and the best books are good for your mind. Your life will be determined by the people you associate with and the books you read. You'll come to love many people you'll meet in books. Read biographies, autobiographies, and history. Books will provide many of the friends, mentors, role models, and heroes you'll need in life. Biographies will help you see there is nothing that can happen to you that wasn't experienced by many who used their failures, disappointments, and tragedies as stepping-stones for a more tremendous life. Many of my best friends are people I've never met: Oswald Chambers, George Mueller, Charles Spurgeon, A. W. Tozer, Abraham Lincoln, Robert E. Lee, François Fénelon, Jean Guyon, and hundreds of others.

Don't read the Bible. Study it. Digest it. Memorize it and realize God's greatest gift to our time on earth is His Word made flesh, living in our hearts through Jesus Christ, our Lord.

What you feed your mind and heart determines your growth as a person.

Forgive. Our unwillingness to forgive when we've been deeply hurt breeds self-pity and bitterness. If you experience God's love and forgiveness through Jesus, you will have no problem in forgiving anyone for anything. The hurt or injustices you experience will leave scars, but your life will be enriched by the joy of practicing what you have received.

Pray. Praying is more than talking to God. Praying is God's Spirit speaking to you and for you and moving you to share your thoughts, problems, and praise with Him. Never allow your unfaithfulness to keep you from praying. God always hears you as you pray in Jesus' name because He is faithful. The

"right" words never matter to God. He hears the words of your heart that can't be expressed in words, and best of all, the Holy Spirit is your interpreter.

Give. Never give to get; give because you have received. Giving is like using a muscle. To be strong, you must exercise "giving" to grow as a person. You can't really enjoy anything without sharing it, including your faith, love, talents, and money. Someday you'll discover we never really give; we are only returning and sharing a small portion of what we've received.

Make decisions. The more decisions you make, the more tremendous your life will be.

Don't wait for the right time. Do something now, today. Don't worry about big decisions. Make many little ones, and the big ones will seem little. Your job is not to make a perfect decision as much as to make a decision and invest your life in making it count.

After choosing to love God, you have only two big decisions in life: your work and your marriage. Don't look for what you like to do. Find something that ought to be done while others are wasting their lives searching for something they would like to do. Don't waste time looking for a better job. Do a better job and you'll have a better job.

Someday you'll meet someone to love and share her life with you. Love between a man and a woman is second only to the love of God, but there is one big difference. God's love never changes, while our love is very changeable. Please remember that commitment in your marriage is more important than love. Commitment will save your marriage when your love dies or until it lives again. I

thought God gave me your grandmother to love me, and she has loved me well, but over the years God has shown me something more. He gave her to me to learn to love, even if she ceased loving me. You can't do this on your own, but you can when you experience the love of Christ. Then and only then will it make sense.

Be thankful. Learning to be thankful covers it all: "In everything give thanks; for this is the will of God in Christ Jesus for you" (1 Thess. 5:18). You may not always be sure of God's will, you may not always be sure that you're doing God's will, but you can easily always be His will by thanking Him for all things.

I hope you'll give thanks for your food with your children as we did with your dad: "Lord, we thank You for our food. But if we had none, we would thank You anyway. Because, Lord, we're not just thankful for what You give us. We are thankful most of all for the privilege of learning to be thankful."

There are hundreds of other thoughts I would love to share with you, but I know God will be revealing them to your heart more wonderfully than any human tongue can tell. Remember:

Learn to laugh at yourself.
Learn to help others laugh.
Learn to laugh when you are up.
Learn to laugh when you are down.
Learn to laugh.

Circumstances won't always allow you to be happy, but Jesus will help you look as if you are.

I love you tremendously,
Your devoted grandfather
Romans 10:17; Acts 20:24

Integrity | Dr. Ted W. Engstrom

President Emeritus, World Vision; Monrovia, California
Written to his grandsons, Jason and Theo

To my very special grandsons,

Some time ago a friend of mine asked me an intriguing question. He asked, "What is the most important ingredient in one's authentic character?"

I thought about that for a long time and came up with a number of answers, but the one that really came home to my mind and heart, and what I want to share with you at this important time in your lives, is the concept of integrity.

The word *integrity* itself is most interesting. I recall taking Latin in high school many years ago, and I learned that the English word *integrity* comes from the Latin word *integritas*. (I really was not much of a Latin student, but I do remember that.) The word *integration* comes from the same root, as does the word *integer*. Basically it means "wholeness" or "completeness" or "consistency."

Integrity in *Webster's Dictionary* is defined as a "strict adherence to a moral set of values." There are at least six of these values: utter sincerity, honesty, candor, not artificial, not shallow, no empty promises.

If you and I take the word *integrity* and reduce it to its simplest terms, we could say that a person of integrity is a man who is a "promise keeper." When he says something, he means it. It can be taken to the bank. That person's word is good.

I don't want to preach to you, but I must tell you that the Bible speaks often of integrity. For example, when Solomon completed the building of the magnificent temple and royal palace, God said to him, "If you walk before Me

Integrity involves not merely acting according to one's beliefs, but acting according to scriptural teaching in the Bible.

in integrity, I will establish your royal throne in Israel forever." The psalmist said, "Let integrity and uprightness preserve me" (Ps. 25:21).

One more Bible quote—Proverbs 11:3: "The integrity of the upright will guide them, but the perversity of the unfaithful will destroy them."

People of integrity can be trusted to be faithful. If they promise something, they will do it. Their actions are built on high moral principles. People of integrity seek to discover what pleases God, and then they do it.

Also, beloved grandsons, integrity has to do with courage. People of integrity stand for their convictions, even at a great personal cost. In the final sense, integrity involves not merely acting according to one's beliefs, but acting according to scriptural teaching in the Bible.

A very special friend of mine has said, "The test of integrity is how you behave when no one is watching." I know that integrity is more easily recognized than defined or analyzed. It is what we do more than what we don't do; it is what we are more than what we are not.

As you know, I really enjoy golf. I have a number of friends who are professional golfers. Tom Watson is a professional golfer—one of the best who ever played the game. He won nearly every major golf tournament at least once and some of them several times. He is respected as well as admired by all who have followed his outstanding career.

Both his skill and his integrity were evident at an early age. He had his heart set on becoming a champion. He also had his personal code of honor firmly in mind.

In the first state tournament he ever entered, he put his putter down behind his ball on one of the greens. To his dismay, the ball moved slightly; no one saw it, of that he was certain. He was under great pressure to win, and there was no time whatever to add up the pluses and minuses of the alternatives. But he knew without hesitation what he must do. He went over to an official and said, "My ball moved." That action cost him a stroke, and he lost the hole. With such action Tom Watson placed his personal integrity ahead of his keen desire to win.

I think you know that Jesus is a supreme model of integrity. His enemies, in their flattery, could only declare, "Teacher, we know that You are true, and teach the way of God in truth" (Matt. 22:16).

There are three ways, if not more, to guard this element in your lives. First of all, guard the inner life. Spend time every day reading at least a portion of the Bible and simply talking to God in your own way about whatever you may be facing, and ask for His help. Tell Him that you love Him.

Second, have a close Christian friend or two who will help monitor your living and actions. Try to be as vulnerable as you can with that trusted friend.

Finally, keep your priorities straight. Remember that God always needs to have first place in your lives. When each of you marries, make sure that your wife is next in your priorities—then whatever children you may have, and then friends. Your work and career, as important as they may be, must always take their place following God and family.

You know that your grandma and I—along with your wonderful parents—love you very much and wish only the best for you in your years ahead. And know that God loves you even more than we do!

Grandma joins me in sending our warm love and appreciation for you. Be all that God intends you to be. God bless you.

Lovingly,
Grandpa

Health and Wholeness | Dan Reiland

Dear Mackenzie and John-Peter,

Health has been a popular, nearly trendy topic for more than a decade, but wholeness is rarely discussed. Health deals largely with the physical realm, and wholeness leans toward the emotional and spiritual realm. The two go hand in hand for a lifestyle that allows you to live to your maximum potential. I'd like to share some thoughts about these two areas.

Laugh often. Laugh every day. Laughter is good for the soul and brings joy to those who laugh with you. Laughter is a great gift to give others. Take God seriously, but don't take yourself seriously. When you think about it, we're all kind of goofy in one way or another. I had a good laugh on myself on a flight to Sacramento. By mistake, I sat in row 13 instead of 14, but obviously I didn't know. A man with a loud voice began to tell me I was sitting in the wrong seat. I proceeded to show him I was in the correct seat. Well, it turned out that the other man was right, and I was wrong. The funny thing is that the other man was completely blind—white-tipped cane and all. The blind guy could find the right seat, but I couldn't. Several other passengers enjoyed the humor in it too!

Play as hard as you work. Working hard is a virtue I believe in, but it is not virtuous to be all work and no play. I have been guilty of this. I still am at times. Play with passion! Your uncle Lan is a fisherman. He loves to fish. He puts everything he has into catching the big one. For him, fishing is pure joy. I prefer ordering mahimahi at a good restaurant, but I'm sure that eating it isn't nearly as much fun as catching it.

Exercise regularly. Exercising requires more than vigorously pulling a movie out of the VCR and shoving in another. But this isn't about looking perfect. No matter how much you chase perfection, you will never achieve it, and it's not important. Your earthly body is only temporary. The reason for exercise is to obtain good health and physical vitality, which will enable you to achieve all God has for you as well as enjoy the life He has given you. Find a sport or exercise you like to do, and do it vigorously three or four times a week. Any more is unnecessary.

Don't believe in diets. They don't work, at least not for the long haul. The sensible formula is simple. Burn more calories than you consume and you lose weight. Consume more calories than you burn and you gain weight. A lifestyle of good nutrition is more important than all the fads and gimmicks put together. Get a couple of good books on nutrition, eat healthy foods in sensible amounts, and every once in a while enjoy a big piece of chocolate cake.

Take time to rest. People who work all the time do not honor God. God designed into our being something called the Sabbath—a day of rest. Take a day each week for rest, a day to break from the regular activities and responsibilities of life and focus on God, family, and friends. Ultimately, wholeness requires a personal relationship with God that is alive, growing, and meaningful. This I pray for you, more than anything else.

Take time to think, talk to God, and smell the roses.

I love you,

Dad

Health and wholeness go hand in hand
for a lifestyle that allows you to
live to your maximum potential.

Perspective | Dr. Ron Jensen

Chairman, Future Achievement International, and High Ground; San Diego, California
Written to his son, Matthew

Dear Matt,

I am rapidly approaching my fiftieth birthday, as you know. And I am using this time to fast and reflect on where my life is and where it needs to be in the years to come.

I am so blessed. I feel that on the one hand, I have seen so many significant things happen in and through me. But on the other hand, I have seen too many times when I have come up short, grieved God, and not been the quality of person God desired me to be.

As I reflect on all of this, I want to pass on to you some of my insights.

I want you to know how proud I am of you—your commitment, love, friendship, excellence, leadership, tenderness, wisdom, zeal, integrity, and overall character. There are growing areas of your life where you have passed me by. That means more to me than you'll ever know.

To aid you in finishing well what you have so outstandingly begun, let me reflect on the word that means more to me every day. That word is *perspective*.

I've concluded that many of my life's successes and failures rotate around my perspective. When I see God properly, view myself rightly, live life thankfully, handle problems appropriately, treat people elegantly, and use time wisely, I win every time. When I lose my perspective, I fail.

As you live out your days, I urge you, dear son, to focus on the right perspective in your life. It helps me to zero in on key words or phrases to do this. You've heard me address some of these but let me pass them on to you

As you live out your days,
I urge you, dear son, to focus on
the right perspective in your life.

in a succinct form. Philippians 3–4 illustrates them well.

First, maintain an eternal perspective of God. The best way to do this is to praise Him. God inhabits the praise of His people. I keep learning that my problems are big when my God is too small. Whenever I enlarge my mental, emotional, and intentional view of God through praise, my big problems become small.

Second, keep affirming yourself. I believe you do this by seeing yourself as God does— forgiven, special, and destined for greatness but

also desperately needy of His power and grace. So, stay broken! Keep depending on Him. This is truly my greatest struggle. I lean into my own strengths and gifts far too often. Whenever I stop trusting God, I miss His best. I long for you to see your God-designed uniqueness through your utter dependence on Him.

Third, handle life by being thankful— always. In everything give thanks. Let the attitude of gratitude flow from your spirit. Thank God for your life, friends, body, opportunities, schooling, family, strangers, the weather, God's creation, and more.

Fourth, face problems head-on by rejoicing. Scott Peck was right—life is difficult. The Phillips translation of James 1:2–4 advises, "Don't resent [problems] as intruders, but welcome them as friends!" I get in trouble every time I handle my stress by seeking anything to ease it other than the Lord by leaning on Him through rejoicing. If you will deliberately rejoice, you'll have joy and impact. As Mother Teresa said, "He who is filled with joy preaches without words."

Fifth, treat people elegantly by edifying them. Keep building people up. Never tear them down. In your thoughts, words, and actions, radically love people. Even when you have to discipline people, do it tenderly because you love them. Francis Schaeffer was right when he wrote, "Christian love and unity is the ultimate apologetic." People will flock to the kingdom when they see our love fleshed out in our biblical relationships with one another.

Finally, dear son and friend, cope with the pressures of life by focusing on what counts.

Oh, how I ache at thinking of the time I have squandered or misspent. Time is a vapor, a mist, a shadow, gone so soon without a trace. Live for eternity. Focus on what will count forever—the Word of God and people. Become mighty in the Word and deeply involved in the lives of people. Share your faith with unbelievers, and build up believers as a way of life. Reproduce leaders who will build others who will do the same. And stay centered in the written and living Word of God.

You are my joy, my love, and much of my legacy, my son. Live your life with God's perspective.

In closing, I leave with you a poem by an anonymous poet that has so deeply moved me over the years:

I counted dollars while God counted crosses.
I counted gains while He counted losses.
I counted my worth by things gained in stores.
He sized me up by the scars that I bore.
I coveted honors and sought degrees.

He wept as He counted the hours on my knees
I never knew until one day by the grave,
How vain are the things that we spend life
　　　to save.

I love you and am so proud of you!
Dad

It has been said that paternity is a career imposed on you without any inquiry into your fitness for it. That is why there are so many fathers who have children, but so few children who have fathers.

Adlai Stevenson

Gratitude | Dan Reiland

Dear Mackenzie and John-Peter,

You met Doug and Sherry Bennett when they visited us last Christmas. They love the Lord, are good friends, and pray for us. I want you to know how special this is and how grateful I am. I will never forget the day when Doug and Sherry flew from Michigan where they live to San Diego to ask me for permission to pray for me and my ministry. I was amazed! But even more than amazed, I was grateful. I was grateful for the generous gift of their prayers for me, my ministry, and my family.

Gratitude is a spirit of the heart that recognizes we get far more than we deserve. You are very fortunate and blessed kids. You can demonstrate gratitude for your blessings by showing a generous spirit toward others. As you get older, this means more than saying a courteous "thank you" to people who have given to you. It may be writing a thoughtful letter, offering words of appreciation and encouragement to them personally, or perhaps helping them accomplish one of their dreams or desires. Gratitude is a response to what others have done for you. Giving is an act that requires initiative on your part. I pray you will make it a life goal to give more than you get.

For many of us this is a challenging goal, for we receive so much. But I can't think of anything more exciting! My delight is in investing in and giving to others. I hope it will be yours too. You will be responsible to pass on what you have received. I am privileged to have received wonderful mentoring in the area of spiritual leadership. I'm so grateful for the opportunity to learn and grow as a leader that I want to pass on what I have learned. God has given me specific people to do this with, such as the Joshua's Men, pastors across the country, and occasionally strangers I may meet along the way. I invest my time in this way out of a grateful heart, and this is the heart I pray for you to possess.

Gratitude helps us understand that we don't travel through life without help from others. When I think of all my friend and mentor John Maxwell has done for me in nearly seventeen years, there is no way I can repay him. I have traveled much farther in life because of his contribution to my personal growth. When I was in my late teen years and early twenties, Ray Crowell invested countless hours in my life; for his wisdom and love, I am so grateful. You will have special people in your life too. Remember them, and know that you don't achieve your dreams alone.

Gratitude helps keep our perspective right by focusing on what we do have rather than what we do not have. When we are not grateful for what we have, we can live shallow and unhappy lives, always wanting more, and never satisfied with what we have. It's like someone buying you an ice-cream cone and wishing you got two scoops rather than one. It never tastes quite as good as when you are grateful for the one you do have!

Be grateful for what you have, remember who helped you get where you are, and think of ways to give to others.

I am grateful that God gave me both of you.

Love,
Dad

You can demonstrate gratitude for your blessings by showing a generous spirit toward others.

Attributes of God | Dr. Bill Bright

Founder and President, Campus Crusade for Christ International; Orlando, Florida

Written to his sons, Zachary and Bradley

My dear, beloved sons, Zac and Brad,
I embrace you not only with the love of a father, but also with the supernatural love of our living Savior who dwells within each one of us. You are very dear to my heart. I love you with all of my being.

The following comments were prompted by a request that I write a letter to my sons as a legacy of the most important lesson I have learned in my entire lifetime. Yet I would prefer that you read this as a personal letter from my heart to yours.

After many years I have come to the conclusion that the most important truth I have ever learned, and therefore the most important truth I could share with each of you, is my growing understanding of the attributes of God.

Our understanding of God determines our lifestyle, choice of friends, literature, and music. Our thoughts, attitudes, motives, desires, and actions are all influenced by our view of God. Our understanding of His attributes determines our love of God and our desire to obey Him.

So I would like for you to consider with me why I love God with every fiber of my being, and why your mother and I have no trouble trusting and obeying Him. I want to share with you just a few of my favorite attributes of God.

First, God is a Person—not just an impersonal force. A person is a conscious, self-aware, volitional being; that is, a being who thinks, who knows, who can make moral choices, and who can have relationships with other persons. This means that God knows us, and we can actually know Him, intimately, and have a relationship with Him.

Second, God is omnipotent, or all-powerful. And all this power has been given to the Son. Jesus said, "All authority has been given to Me in heaven and on earth" (Matt. 28:18). He spoke and the entire universe—one hundred billion or more galaxies—came into existence (Heb. 11:3). If He desired, He could speak another one hundred billion galaxies into existence tomorrow! Nothing is too difficult for Him.

Third, God is omnipresent, or present everywhere. He is Spirit and not captive to the space-time dimension in which we find ourselves. How comforting to know that He is with us everywhere we go—work, play, school, in airplanes, on highways, or wherever. The psalmist reminded us of this point: "If I ascend into heaven, You are there; if I make my bed in hell, behold, You are there" (Ps. 139:8).

Fourth, God is omniscient, or all-knowing, and all-wise. There is nothing He does not know. His Word says, "God is greater than our heart, and knows all things" (1 John 3:20). He is aware of everything—our thoughts, our deeds, even the number of hairs on our heads. "Oh, the depth of the riches

To know our Lord is to love Him. When we truly love Him, our desire will be to obey and follow Him.

both of the wisdom and knowledge of God!" (Rom. 11:33).

Fifth, God is sovereign. He not only has all power; He can do anything anytime and anywhere He pleases. Nothing can stop Him, not even what we call "the laws of physics." He created them, and He can bend them or break them whenever He likes. We serve a sovereign God for whom miracles are routine. As Jesus said, "With God all things are possible" (Mark 10:27).

Sixth, God is holy. He is pure and perfect, without flaw, without iniquity. The Bible says, "Exalt the LORD our God, and worship at His holy hill; for the LORD our God is holy" (Ps. 99:9).

Seventh, God is truth—absolute truth. The Bible reveals that He cannot lie: "Every word of God is pure" (Prov. 30:5). Truth is a Person, not a concept. Jesus said, "I am . . . the truth" (John 14:6). This is extremely important. It means God and His Word can always be trusted—without exception.

Eighth, God is righteous. He is morally pure, and all that emanates from Him, including His laws and actions, is morally pure and right: "Righteous are You, O LORD, and upright are Your judgments" (Ps. 119:137).

Ninth, God is just. He always does the right and fair thing. For example, sin must always be punished, with no exception, or else God would be unjust and inconsistent and would deny His very nature. Is there a conflict between God's just nature and His loving nature, which is the tenth attribute? By no means. The reconciliation of these two attributes is the most wonderful truth of the universe! "He is the Rock, His work is perfect; for all His ways are justice . . . righteous and upright is He" (Deut. 32:4).

Tenth, "God is love" (1 John 4:8). For the punishment of man's sin, God's just nature was fully satisfied by His love nature. Because of His love, in the greatest and most astounding act of love in all history, He decided to take the punishment for all of our sins upon Himself! "God demonstrates His own love toward us, in that while we were still sinners, Christ died for us" (Rom. 5:8).

Eleventh, God is merciful and compassionate. God's mercy and compassion, combined with His love, caused Him to redeem us from eternal death by shedding His own blood. The psalmist declared, "Great are Your tender mercies, O LORD" (Ps. 119:156). And His mercy was not a one-time event: "His compassions . . . are new every morning" (Lam. 3:22–23).

Twelfth, God is faithful. He always keeps His covenants, or promises—without fail. "He remembers His covenant forever, the word which He commanded, for a thousand generations" (Ps. 105:8).

Thirteenth, God never changes. He is always the same. He assures us, "I am the LORD, I do not change" (Mal. 3:6). The Bible also says, "Jesus Christ is the same yesterday, today, and forever" (Heb. 13:8). We can trust that tomorrow His attributes will be exactly the same as they are today.

These are just a few attributes of our infinite God with whom we shall spend all eternity, getting to know Him better and better, forever and ever, without end. Praise His holy name.

We are commanded to love, trust, and obey God, but unless we truly know Him and understand His attributes with the enabling of the Holy Spirit, we are incapable of doing this. To know our Lord is to love Him. When we truly love Him, our desire will be to obey and follow Him.

Understanding the attributes of God is the most important lesson I have learned. I want to leave this good word as a legacy to you.

With special love.

Yours for fulfilling the Great Commission in this generation,

Dad

Make a Heart Connection | Dan Reiland

Dear Mackenzie,

You are ten years old today. Happy birthday! You are more precious to me than words can ever express, and I love you with all my heart. Ten years ago today you came into this world and changed my life forever. I thought I understood love as much as anyone could. But that morning when I held you in my arms and heard you cry for the first time, tears of joy rolled down my face. I loved you from the very first second more deeply than I knew possible. No classroom could teach in a year what I learned from your presence in that moment. In that moment the love I felt for you helped me discover a deeper place of connection—a heart connection.

Far too many people live life without ever being fully connected to others at a heart level. Whether it be with their children, friends,

spouse, or even at times a stranger—life is meant to be lived close to people.

People live fast these days, but they don't live deep. They live at the surface, like a rock skipping over the surface of a lake. The trip may be fun, but it will be short-lived. Many live at a near frantic pace, but the things of the heart, the things that are truly important in life, only come by slowing down. Playing a game of checkers, eating an ice-cream cone, throwing a ball for a puppy, watching a sunset with your best friend, or laughing, really laughing together until our sides hurt and tears roll down our cheeks—that's connecting.

When you and I play one-on-one basketball, we connect. I love playing not just because I can slam-dunk your eight-foot basket, but because I can see every fiber in you playing your absolute best. It's usually cold, really cold. Your nose is red and my ears are freezing, but it doesn't matter. The more I cheer you on and encourage you, the better you play. Nothing is quite like it.

When I read you stories at night just before your bedtime, we connect—just you and me. Those are the times when you giggle and smile, tell me about school, and pray for sweet dreams. Those are some of the most cherished moments, connected moments, ones I carry in my heart.

When we wrestle on the floor, we connect. It's usually with your brother, too, and that makes it even more fun, although you two have been ganging up on me lately. You laugh so hard, I think you will explode!

Knowing people isn't connecting. Talking with people isn't connecting. Having many friends isn't connecting. Spending time with friends doesn't guarantee connecting. Connecting is about looking in someone's eyes and knowing who he is and that he cares. It's knowing he is there for you, and trust isn't an issue.

Some things block a heart connection. Fear blocks a heart connection. The only thing to fear in life is your mom's chili. That will scare anyone! Other than that, God will get you through. Some fear is natural and needed, but most is completely unnecessary. If you're

Whether it be with your children, friends, spouse, or even at times a stranger— life is meant to be lived close to people.

afraid of something, slow down, think it through, and do something about it. I'm afraid of spiders. Dumb, huh, but I am. If I slow down, think it through, and then just stomp that furry critter, everything is okay again.

Insecurity blocks a heart connection. All people have insecurities, maybe about how they look, what they can or can't do, or even what family they belong to. The important thing is to think about yourself as God would, nothing more and nothing less. God doesn't love you because you're valuable; you're valuable because He loves you. Remember that rag doll Mommy has? Muffin? She's had it for nearly thirty years, and it looks it! Muffin is falling apart at the seams, one eye is missing, and there are several holes in the doll. The logical thing to do is to throw it out because it has no value, but that is unthinkable. The rag doll has immeasurable value to your mom. She loves it. Why? Muffin means so much to her because it represents precious memories, history, and

moments of connection. Mommy doesn't love the rag doll because it's valuable; the rag doll is valuable because she loves it. It's the same with you and God. You are valuable because of God's love in you and for you, and God never changes.

Lack of desire blocks a heart connection. Connecting deeply with others takes initiative and effort. You must want to be close to people, or you will miss out on the best life has to offer. Every day when you wake up, I hope you think of someone special and ask yourself how you can connect with him.

Let me share with you a few things that will help you connect with others. I've given you a clue to three of them. First, you must not be afraid; just go for it. Yes, rejection and hurt might come your way, but the risk is worth it. Second, think well of yourself. You can't give to others what you don't possess inside yourself. In other words, be yourself. That's when you are at your best. Third, take the initiative. Be the one to step out and make the first move. If it's someone you are upset with, make the first move anyway. Life is too short to miss out. Fourth, listen with more than just your ears. Listen with your eyes and heart. Look deep and touch the heart. And last, have fun! Parts of this letter may sound serious, but the point is joy.

What I want most for you is a life of inner joy that comes from being connected at a heart level with the people you love and care for the most.

Love,
Dad

Spiritual Heritage | Dr. Elmer Towns

Dean, School of Religion, Liberty University; Lynchburg, Virginia
Written to his son, Stephen ("Sam")

Dear Sam,

Last week your son was born, my grandson! Congratulations!

Thank you for naming him Bradford Elmer Towns, preserving my name, Elmer Towns, in heritage and name. Although we will call him Brad, thank you for the honor of choosing his middle name after me. When Brad thinks about his middle name, Elmer, I hope that he remembers some of the things that were important to his grandfather.

First, I want Bradford Elmer Towns to

remember that I was a dedicated follower of Jesus Christ. Remind him that his great-grandmother and great-grandfather met at a dance and spent their young lives as "flappers," meaning that they ran to the dances and the bars but had no time for God. A door-to-door salesman came by Great-grandmother Towns's home in Savannah, Georgia, selling coffee. He asked me where I went to Sunday school, and he ended up taking me to Eastern Heights Presbyterian Church. Because Great-grandmother Towns had such a firm commitment to character—she was a farm girl—she

Remind Brad of my Christian heritage and lead him to Jesus Christ, as I led you to Jesus Christ.

sent me to Sunday school and I did not miss a single time in fourteen years. I learned the Bible, which had an impact on my life. I learned the Westminster Shorter Catechism and the sovereignty of God. Because of that Christian heritage, I was born again on July 25, 1950, after attending a revival meeting in Savannah. Remind Brad of my Christian heritage and lead him to Jesus Christ, as I led you to Jesus Christ.

Second, remind Bradford Elmer Towns that his namesake was a hard worker. I told the story in an early book, *Stories on the Front Porch*, that I learned to work hard as a young boy cutting grass. My buddies were in a plowed field playing tackle football; I was mowing the lawn. When we got finished, we were all filthy and washed with a hose on our lawn. We were all tired, and we lay around and talked. Something happened that day—I changed my mind about work. I decided that I could have as much fun when I worked hard as when I played hard; and that attitude about work was important. I had a new attitude about work, which changed my life.

Third, tell Bradford Elmer Towns that the name Towns is important. His great-grandmother, Erin Towns, used to take me and my sister to Sardinia, South Carolina, where there was a large granite family stone marking the location of her ancestors in the family graveyard. She stood me and my sister in front of the large ten-foot family stone and said to us, "You are a Towns. Be proud of that name." But she did not stop there. She said, "You are a Towns. Make me proud of you."

And still she did not stop there. Then she said, "You are a Towns. You can do what you've got to do." That last statement became a driving force in my life. Many times when I told her I couldn't do something, such as I could not push my bike to the service station to get air in the tire, I was too tired to deliver my papers, or it was raining too hard to go to school, she said to me, "You can do what you've got to do."

Sam, I would like to pass a lesson from Grandmother Towns through you to Bradford, "Learn it once and live by it the rest of your life: you can do what you've got to do."

Remind Bradford Elmer Towns to be a man of the Book. My prayer for Brad is that he might be in the center of God's will. Remind Bradford Elmer Towns that the power of my life was Jesus Christ, and for him to let Jesus Christ live in his heart and work through him. My life verse has been Galatians 2:20: "I have been crucified with Christ; it is no longer I who live, but Christ lives in me; and the life which I now live in the flesh I live by faith in the Son of God, who loved me and gave Himself for me." The driving force in my life has been the "indwelling Christ." If Brad will ask Christ to come into his heart, then let the "indwelling Christ" motivate him, he will accomplish much for God.

Tell Bradford Elmer Towns that family is important. His great-great-great-grandfather was Robert E. Lee MacFadden (1837–1912). He did not smoke, drink, or curse. He claimed to be the best speller of normal words in South Carolina, and he was an elder in the local Presbyterian church. When the quarter-time minister did not show or was not scheduled to show, Robert E. Lee MacFadden said he could not preach, but he could expound the Word of God for up to one hour. He owned five slave families, and contrary to law, he taught their children to read and write. Every evening he had them up to the plantation house where he read the Scriptures, expounded the Scriptures up to one hour, and had evening prayers with them. He made them go to church on Sunday. When he went off to the Civil War, he prayed that he might not needlessly kill anyone or be killed. When he came home, he gave each slave family five acres of ground, and he set up a bookkeeping system so that others might not steal from them or they might not steal from others. I have a hunch that Robert E. Lee MacFadden prayed for me, three generations away; for you, Sam, four generations away; and for Bradford Elmer Towns, five generations away. Family is important.

Remember to tell Brad that he is a Towns; make us proud. Remember that he is a Towns; he can do what he has got to do.

Sincerely yours,

Your dad

No Regrets | Dan Reiland

Dear Mackenzie and John-Peter,

Your grammy died last year in February. It was so unexpected. A stroke took her life as easily and quickly as blowing out a candle. She slipped into a coma and never woke up. There was no time to say good-bye. There was no time to do anything except respond to the immediate sense of loss.

John and Margaret Maxwell flew across the country to comfort us and help us process the shock. John talked about how special Grammy Betty was to all of us at her memorial service. It felt like a warm and reverent party celebrating how wonderful she was. I couldn't help thinking when the Scottish piper played "Amazing Grace" that she should be there with us. I thought to myself, *Mom, I wish you were here to see how much everyone loved you!* What a strange thought! Grief can do that, I guess. She couldn't be there, and

there would never again be a chance to tell her how special she was or tell her anything at all.

I have few regrets in life, perhaps only one. My mom and I, though our relationship was good, had not expressed deeper and more candid thoughts and feelings with each other. I cannot change this regret.

Two nights ago another unexpected event ended the lives of twelve people who were sleeping, possibly just before their alarm clocks went off. An unexpected tornado hit northern Georgia less than fifty miles from our house. It came so quickly, there was no chance to warn victims to try to get to a safe place. So much destruction!

The tornado came like a thief in the night and robbed friends and family forever of the most precious gift—life itself. It reminded me of your grammy, and I wondered if those who lost their lives were told the night before how special they were by a friend or loved one. I wonder if there were any regrets.

I learned a lesson that I want to pass on to you. Live without regrets.

Regrets come from morsels of life that are not lived. Every second of life is a gift from God. You can't buy one more hour, so live to the fullest every moment you have been given. I don't mean that you should never relax or enjoy some quiet downtime, but I do mean that you shouldn't waste the precious gift of time.

Regrets come from not trying new things. I remember thinking that acupunc-

ture was for crazy people. Who wants to be a human pin cushion? Then a wonderful friend of mine named Michele Hardin talked me into trying acupuncture since I had found no relief for severe allergies and an acute sinus condition through conventional medicine. The results were incredible. I could breathe as I never had before.

Regrets come from ignoring God when He whispers to your spirit. God often prompts me to pray. Many of my most fulfilling moments in life are in response to those promptings. I miss out on God's best when I do not respond to His promptings.

You can't buy one more hour, so live to the fullest every moment you have been given.

Regrets come from broken relationships that are not mended. Life is too short to leave relationships like puzzle pieces scattered in a closet. Put the puzzle together so that you can enjoy the picture as it was designed to be. Tend to your relationships as if they were roses in a prized rose garden. Proper care and feeding will produce beautiful results.

Regrets come from not telling your friends and family what you really think and feel. I remember sitting down to a meal with Uncle Nick and Aunt Sherry. It was stuffed bell peppers. I would not have fed them to a starving goat. I don't know what they were stuffed with, but I was sure I would need to stop by the Emergency Room to have my stomach pumped. When Aunt Sherry asked how I liked them, not wanting to hurt her feelings, I raved about how delicious they were. I soon started feeling so bad, I considered calling Life Flight. As it was, nature took care of the stomach pumping for me. It wasn't a pretty sight. We returned several

months later, and can you guess? Yup, stuffed peppers again! I had a choice: dial 911 or tell her what I really thought. Doing that was much more difficult because I had not the first time. I was ready to receive her crushed spirit, but she laughed and said, "Your uncle Nick hates them too. I just made them again because I thought you liked them so much." I had a peanut butter and jelly sandwich and can't remember when a meal tasted so good.

There are deeper and more important things in life than bell peppers, but the principle is nonetheless vital. Say what is on your mind, but say it kindly and lovingly.

Regret comes when God places opportunity in your hand and you let it slip through your fingers like drops of cool water. For any of life's regrets, God's grace is available and sufficient, but you can never go back and do it over again.

My dear Mackenzie and John-Peter, live without regrets. Live each moment to its fullest. I don't know how many days God has given you, but my prayer concerning the important things in life is that you seldom, if ever, must look over your shoulder and wish you could do it over again differently.

Laugh often, love much, and tell people what you really think and feel.

Love,

Dad

There is just one way to bring up a
child in the way he should go,
and that is to travel that way yourself.

Abraham Lincoln

About the Author

DAN REILAND is vice president of leadership and church development for INJOY Ministries, with a primary role in church consulting. Dan has fifteen years of pastoral experience in the local church and a heart for family life. He and his wife, Patti, and their two children, Mackenzie and John-Peter, reside in Atlanta, Georgia. Dan is the author of *Shoulder to Shoulder: Strengthening Your Church by Supporting Your Pastor.*